SHANGHAI MUSEUM

SHANGHAI MUSEUM

Edited by Chen Xiejun

Shanghai Museum
In collaboration with
London Editions, Hong Kong

Contents

Editor (Shanghai): Chen Xiejun
Editor (London): Susan Whitfield
Executive editors (Shanghai): Wang Yuntian, Liu Jie
Co-ordinating editors: Antony White, Cui Jing
English translation: Haiyao Zheng
French translation: Colette Lahary-Gautié
Design: Anikst Design, London
Printed by Zhejiang HK Graphics and Printing Ltd
Text and images: ©2007 The Shanghai Museum
This edition ©2007 London Editions (HK) Ltd
ISBN: 978-7-80017-858-0/J · 750
First published in 2007 by
Great Wall Publishers

Distributed outside China:
By Scala Publishers Limited
Northburgh House, 10 Northburgh Street,
London EC1V OAT
United Kingdom
Tel: 44 (0) 20 7490 9900

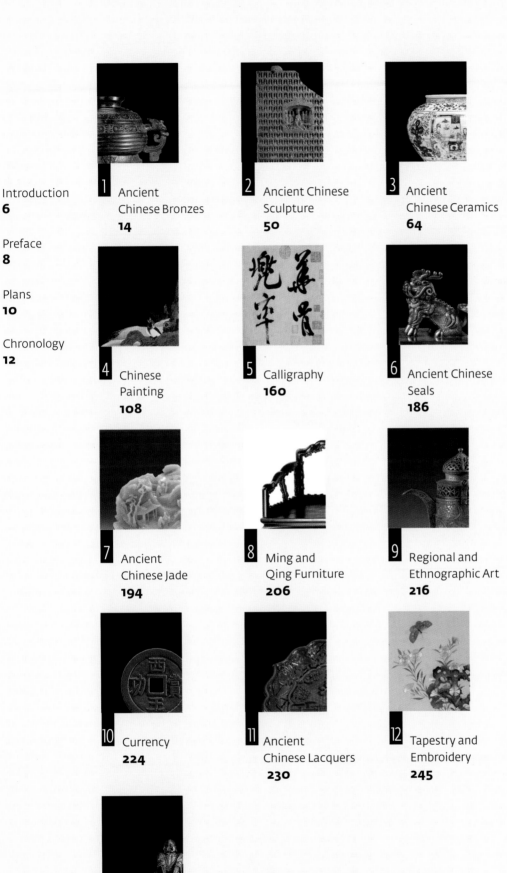

INTRODUCTION

The Shanghai Museum, established in 1952, is a leading museum of pre-modern Chinese art. In the 1990s a new building was commissioned. It was designed by the architect Xing Tonghe and opened to the public on October 12th 1996. 39,200 square metres in size, the building has a circular top on a square base, symbolizing Chinese cosmology, 'the square earth under the round sky'. The building skilfully combines traditional Chinese culture with modern design.

The museum has ten galleries for permanent collections and three temporary exhibition spaces jointly comprising over 10,000 square metres. 120,000 of the close to a million items in the collection (excluding coins) are outstanding pieces renowned throughout the world. They date from the Neolithic to the beginning of the twentieth century. The Museum is especially celebrated for its collections of bronzes, ceramics, calligraphy and paintings, displayed in four galleries. The other six permanent galleries show sculpture, seals, jade, furniture, coins and regional and ethnographic art. International exhibitions are held in the other three galleries.

The museum staff includes specialists in research, authentication, archaeology, museum management, education, cultural exchange and exhibitions. The museum publishes more than ten academic books and exhibition catalogues every year and also produces three scholarly journals. The museum also has a library, a conservation science laboratory and conservation studios. There is a multi-media auditorium for international conferences, equipped with simultaneous translation and film projection facilities.

Foreword

Epitomizing China's ancient civilization and rich cultural heritage, bronze artifacts have been treasured items ever since the time of the Shang and Zhou aristocrats for whom they were made. Ritual bronzes served as ceremonial offerings to ancestors, as banquet utensils, and occasionally as formal gifts. Members of China's nobility possessed sets of bronzes, the sizes and types of which conveyed the social status of their owners.

Bronze Age artisans mastered complex casting techniques and produced vessels with rich decoration. In the period from the fifth to the third century BC,China's Iron Age began, but the metal industry was still dominated by bronze casting.

Many bronzes have been found in the border areas of China. Characterized by distinctive shapes and local styles, these bronzes exhibit the artistic achievements of minority peoples living in the border areas, and they also supply valuable evidence of cultural exchanges among the different nationalities of ancient China.

前　言

中国商周时代青铜器是古代社会文明的重要标志，它是物质生产的造成社会的礼制的特殊产物。当时期青铜器最主要，礼仪文化，祭祝宝器等活动中的青铜器最大宗，不见身价的出征。将有与他们相映衬的礼器，众多前各式记载的公元前三世纪是早期铁器时代。战时两项副技术的青铜器仍在建设成果，石次花里来社的特点。青铜器种类的最多，几乎包括那些。陶治技术的完善是表力对生产技术。这铜及地区，发现了许多具有鲜特色的造型和独特的地方风格的青铜器与交错的铸造遗物，众多的青铜器，显示了这些各族青铜技术的成就。

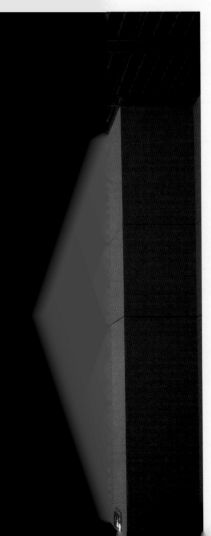

PREFACE

The Shanghai Museum was established in 1952. After five decades of hard work it has now become a world-class museum. Dedicated to pre-modern Chinese art, it has a collection of almost one million objects, 120,000 of which are exquisite masterpieces. They cover twenty-one categories, including ancient bronzes, ceramics, calligraphy, painting, sculpture, ivory, bamboo and wood carving, lacquer, oracle bones, seals and furniture. Among them, the bronze, ceramic, calligraphy and painting collections are especially celebrated.

The ancient bronze collection covers all forms and all periods, reflecting the history and development of ancient Chinese bronzes between the 18th to 7th centuries BC. The ceramics collection contains masterpieces from all the major kilns, from the exquisitely carved earthenwares of Liangzhu Neolithic culture through stonewares and then porcelain from the Tang and Song period to the products of the Jingdezhen imperial kiln in the Ming and Qing periods. The collection therefore covers the complete history of Chinese ceramics and is renowned around the world for its quality. The calligraphy and painting collections are said to comprise half the total collection from Southern China. The calligraphic masterpieces include *The Yatouwan Letter* by Wang Xianzhi, *The Thousand Character Classic* by Gao Xian and *The Kusun Letter* by Huaisu. Paintings such as Sun Wei's *Hermits* and Liang Kai's *Eight Eminent Monks* are world treasures while the Ming and Qing painting collections are unsurpassed.

Items from the other categories are also quite superb. The furniture gallery contains pieces from two great masters, Wang Shixiang and Chen Mengjia. There are also large collections of coins, jades, seals and sculptures replete with important items, giving a complete view of all historical periods. It is rare to see regional and ethnographic art represented in an art museum, but the Shanghai Museum believes in an open and inclusive approach.

Most of the pieces were purchased with government funds and some have travelled through many hands and many lands before returning to China. Some items have been graciously donated by private collectors or generous museum supporters. There are a small number of exchange items from sister museums and archaeological pieces acquired directly from excavation. Although the history of each acquisition is different, all have survived through many changes which have left their mark. Thus each item bears evidence of the historical periods through which it has passed.

The Shanghai Museum collection reflects the achievement of Chinese culture and art from earliest times and is an immensely rich source of information. I hope this catalogue truly reflects and embodies the collection's worth and that the charm of the items will reach across time and space to move and enlighten people with their singular beauty.

Chen Xiejun
Director of Shanghai Museum

PLANS

Ground floor

1 Ancient Chinese Bronze Gallery
2 Ancient Chinese Sculpture Gallery
3 No. 1 Exbition Hall
4 High Definition Graphics Hall
5 Museum Shop
6 Museum Restaurant

First floor

1 Ancient Chinese Ceramic Gallery
2 Zande Lou Ceramic Gallery
3 No. 2 Exbition Hall
4 Tearoom

Second floor

1 Chinese Painting Gallery
2 Chinese Calligraphy Gallery
3 Chinese Seal Gallery

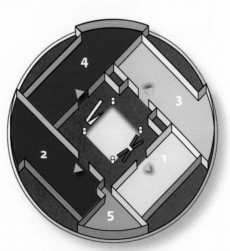

Third floor

1 Ancient Chinese Jade Gallery
2 Chinese Ming and Qing Furniture Gallery
3 Chinese Minority Nationalities' Art Gallery
4 Chinese Coin Gallery
5 No. 3 Exhibition Hall

12,000 - 2,000 B.C Neolithic Age	Chinese Neolithic civilization flourished c.2500 B.C.	Indo European empires in Asia Minor flourished c.2500 B.C.
2070 - 1600B.C Xia Dynasty	First bronze vessels cast c. 1700 B.C.	Use of sail on seagoing vessels in the Aegean c. 2,000 B.C.
c.1600 - 1046 B.C Shang Dynasty Bronze Age	Chinese script first in use c.1400 B.C. Earliest surviving Chinese literature c.1000 B.C. Beginning of urban life c.1600 B.C. Iron technology introduced c. 650 B.C.	Phoenicians develop alphabetic script c.1100 B.C.
1046 - 221 B.C Zhou Dynasty Iron Age begins in China	551 - 479 B.C. Confucius 372 - 289 B.C. Mencius	776 B.C first Olympic Games held in Greece 753 B.C. Traditional founding of Rome c. 560 B.C Siddhartha Gautama, founder of Buddhism, born in India 429 - 347 B.C. Plato 384 - 321 B.C. Aristotle 356 - 323 B.C. Alexander the Great
221 - 206 B.C Qin Dynasty	221 - 207 B.C. Unification of Chinese Empire, law, roads and language Qin Warrior Army Mausoleum begun 221 B.C.	
206 B.C to A.D 220 Han Dynasty	Daoism flourishes Opening of the 'Silk Road' across Central Asia linking China to the West c.112 B.C. Buddhism reaches China c. A.D.150	c. A.D. 30 Jesus of Nazareth, founder of Christianity, crucified in Jerusalem AD. 117 Roman Empire at its greatest extent
220 - 280 Three Kingdoms	Magnetic compass in use 271	238 Gothic invasion of the Roman Empire
265 - 420 Jin Dynasty	285 Confucianism introduced into Japan Beginning of the construction of the Great Canal c.300	330 The capital of Roman Empire transferred to Constantinople.
386 - 589 North-South Dynasty		
589 - 618 Sui Dynasty	606 Creation of written examinations Completion of Great Canal	

618 - 907 Tang Dynasty	The Chinese empire reaches its greatest extent until the 18th century. Chinese culture, language and politics dominate the Far East c. 660 Golden Age of Chinese poetry Printing invented in China Porcelain technique invented c. 700 755 The An Lushan rebellion. The withdrawal of China from Central Asia	632 Death of Mohammed, founder of Islam; beginning of Arab expansion Spread of Islam to Turkestan and the Tarim Basin c.755 800 Charlemagne, King of the Franks, crowned emperor in Rome; beginning of the new western empire later to be known as the Holy Roman Empire
907 - 960 The Five Dysnasties		
960 - 1127 Northern Song Liao in North	961 Liao capital established at Beijing Khitans overrun northern China, establish Liao dynasty and capital at Beijing Great Age of Chinese painting, ceramics and printing	1066 Norman conquest of England 1096 First Crusade: Franks invade Anatolia and Syria and found crusader states First universities in Europe c.1100
1127 - 1279 Southern Song Jin Ruzhen in North	1275 Marco Polo arrives in China	1241 Mongols invade Poland, Hungary and Bohemia 1299 Ottoman Turks begin expansion in Anatolia
1279 - 1368 Yuan (Mongols)	1279 Gunpowder invented 1264 Mongol conquest	
1368 - 1644 Ming	1381 Yongle put in charge of Beiping garrison 1402 Yongle wins empire 1420 Yongle transfers capital from Nanjing to Beijing 1420 Chinese fleet in Africa	1445 Johannes Gutenberg prints first book in Europe 1453 Ottoman Turks capture Constantinople; end of Byzantine Empire 1492 Columbus reaches America Italian Renaissance c.1500 1521 Suleiman the Magnificent, Ottoman sultan, conquers Belgrade 1526 Babur founds Mughal dynasty 1564 - 1616 Shakespeare, poet and dramatist Scientific Revolution begins in Europe c.1610
1644 - 1912 Qing (Manchu)	1839 - 1842 Opium war: Britain annexes Hong Kong 1851 - 1864 Taiping Rebellion in China	Age of European Enlightenment c. 1760 1776 American Declaration of Independence 1789 French Revolution begins 1815 Congress of Vienna 1848 Communist Manifesto issued by Marx and Engels 1905 Einstein's theory of relativity 1917 Russian Revolution

ANCIENT CHINESE BRONZES

Bronze work is among the most outstanding of the ancient arts of China. The casting, decoration and inscriptions are exceptional, unrivalled by bronzes from any other ancient civilisation. The Chinese Bronze Age started in the 18th century BC and lasted for 1500 years to the late Zhou. Early bronzes were intimately linked with the religious and political structures of their time as, aside from weapons, they were designed and made for sacrificial and other ritual ceremonies. The designs are strong and distinctive. Different forms and quantities of the bronzes were allowed for use by different ranks of the nobility, and their designs are strong and distinctive. The kings, princes and nobles for whom the bronzes were made often had accounts of family and personal events inscribed on them, thereby ensuring the preservation of important historical information. Over the course of the Bronze Age, the forms, decoration and inscriptions varied under different rulers, in different locations. Because of the individual tastes of the patrons ancient Chinese bronzes are unrivalled in their variety and splendour.

The Shanghai Museum has one of the richest collections of ancient Chinese bronzes in the world. Comprising 7000 pieces of the highest quality covering all forms and periods the collection offers a comprehensive view of ancient bronze history. It also includes many national treasures such as the famous *Da Ke Ding* (see catalogue 29). ZHOU YA

1

1 Waisted *jue* (ritual wine vessel)

Erlitou period (18th – 16th century BC)
Length from spout to point 14.1 cm
Height 11.7 cm

Jue are among the earliest of the excavated bronzes. They appeared in the Erlitou period but are most common in the succeeding Shang period. They come in two basic forms. The earlier is more unformed and resembles the pottery *jue* that preceded bronzes. It has three short legs extending outwards from the body and it does not have a post on the mouth. The second shape is more refined, with a slender body, and a narrower and straighter mouth usually with a post. The three legs are longer, also extending outwards from the body.

This pre-Shang bronze belongs to the first type. It is waisted, oval in section, with a flat bottom, narrow spout and short point. It stands on a tripod of three conical, thin and short legs that extend outwards from the body. Like many early bronzes, the sides of this *jue* are thin and it is roughly made. Traces of clay are visible inside the chiselled areas, indicating that it was made using a clay mould. This was the primary casting technique used during the Chinese Bronze Age.
MA JINHONG

2

2 Rectangular axe head with inlaid cross design
Erlitou period (18th – 16th century BC)
Length 35.6 cm

3 *Ding* (food container) with *taotie* design
Early Shang period (16th – mid-15th century BC)
Diameter 16 cm
Height 19.4 cm

3

4 *Hu* (wine flask) with inscription 'X'

Mid-Shang period
(mid-15th – 13th century BC)
Diameter 5 cm
Height 25.3 cm

4

5 *Jia* (wine vessel) with *taotie* design
Mid-Shang period (mid-15th – 13th century BC)
Diameter of mouth 18.4
Height 31.1 cm

The *jia*, a ritual vessel, is assumed to have been used to heat wine both because of its shape and also because many excavated *jia* contain traces of smoke and burn marks on their bases and white scale inside (the remnants of wine). Bronze *jia* appeared pre-Shang but matured during the Shang period.

This *jia* has a large body, a flared wide lip with two mushroom-shaped square posts. It has a long neck and lobed belly, resting on three conical legs. There is an arched handle between the neck and the belly. Most mid-Shang *jia* have necks and bodies divided into registers and flat bottoms and it is therefore rare to see a *jia* with a lobed belly such as this.

The square posts are decorated with flame patterns. The neck and belly are decorated with a mask design (known as *taotie*), the design on the neck bordered by a band of small circles and the *taotie* on the belly have large protruding eyes. Although this decoration is ubiquitous on bronzes of this period, this is the only *jia* from the period with this kind of design. MA JINHONG

5

6   *Jue* (wine vessel) with inscription '*jia*'
Late Shang period
(13th – 11th century BC)
Length from spout to point 16.8 cm
Height 21 cm

7   *Gu* (wine vessel) with inscription '*huang*'
Late Shang period
(13th – 11th century BC)
Diameter 16 cm
Height 27.3 cm

6

7

8

9

8 *Zun* (wine vessel) with inscription *'zhui fu gui'*

Late Shang period (13th – 11th century BC)
Diameter 23.8 cm
Height 31.3 cm

9 *Jia* (wine vessel) with *taotie* design

Late Shang period (13th – 11th century BC)
Diameter 22.6 cm
Height 48.2 cm

10 *You* **(wine vessel) with inscription** *'yue fu'*
Late Shang period
(13th – 11th century BC)
Mouth 13.7 × 15 cm
Height 33.3 cm

11 *Fang yi* **(wine container) with inscription** *'ding'*
Late Shang period
(13th – 11th century BC)
Mouth 13.1 × 9.7 cm
Height 21.3 cm

11

10

12

12 *Gong* (wine vessel) with inscription *Gong Fu Yi*

Late Shang period (13th – 11th century BC)
Length 31.5 cm, Height 29.5 cm

Gong, a ritual wine vessel, comes in two forms. Either the whole vessel is shaped like an animal, often an ox or ram, or the lid of the vessel is shaped as a mythical creature while the body is jug-shaped with a ring foot. This piece belongs to the second type. The front of the lid is an animal head with horns, pricked ears and round eyes. The back of the lid is shaped like an ox head, also with pricked ears. On the central ridge of the lid is a small dragon carved in relief, with a long body and curled tail. Both sides of the dragon are decorated with phoenix patterns and in front of each phoenix is a small snake. The overall decoration of the body is also comprised of phoenix patterns, dominated on each side by a large phoenix in profile with a protruding eye, a curved beak and long elegant crest. The claws of the phoenix rest on the ring foot. There is an ox-shaped handle on the back. Both the lid and body of the vessel bear the same three-character inscription: *'gong fu yi'*. The vessel is exquisitely cast and decorated, making it an outstanding piece.

MA JINHONG

13 *Lei* **(large wine vessel) with**
taotie **design**
Late Shang period
(13th – 11th century BC)
Diameter of mouth 18.6 cm
Height 43.5 cm

13

14 *Fang lei* (large wine vessel) made for *Ya Hu*

Late Shang period (13th – 11th century BC)
Mouth 20.1 × 17.2 cm
Height 53 cm

The *lei* is a large ritual wine vessel. This is a *fang lei* – having a rectangular cross-section – and weighs almost 30 kg. There are two animal-shaped handles on the shoulder, another on the lower part of the belly. The vessel has six registers of relief decoration. Bird designs appear on the mouth, the top half of the belly and the foot. The shoulder is decorated with dragon designs. *Taotie* designs cover the middle and lower of the body with long curled horns and sharp clawed feet. The designs are in high relief against a background of fine cloud and thunder patterns. The protruding patterns are decorated with intaglio lines and the broad flanges are lightened with grooves. There is an inscription inside recording that this vessel was made for Ya Hu, an eminent family of the time.

Ancient Chinese bronze art reached its peak in the late Shang period and is exemplified by this *lei* with its heavy body and complex design. MA JINHONG

14

15

15 *Ding* (ritual tripod for food) with dragon pattern
Late Shang period
(13th – 11th century BC)
Diameter of mouth 24.2 cm
Height 31.1 cm

16 *Pou* (wine vessel) with four rams' heads
Late Shang period
(13th – 11th century BC)
Diameter of mouth 31.6 cm
Height 38.8 cm

16

17 *Fang zun* (large wine vessel) made for Gui Gu

Early Western Zhou (11th century BC)
Diameter of mouth 20.1 cm
Height 21.8 cm

The *zun* is a large or medium size ritual wine vessel which first appeared in the Shang and continued in use until the Warring States period. The shouldered square belly form of *zun* seen here was gradually replaced by a taller cylindrical form by the late Shang. This piece, which dates from later, was therefore made deliberately to emulate an ancient style. It has curved openwork flanges. The neck is decorated with banana leaf shaped *taotie* above pairs of phoenix. The design on the sides of the narrow shoulder is a diagonal two-headed dragon, while *taotie* designs also dominate the belly and there are pairs of phoenix on each side of the foot. All these are raised against a background of fine thunder patterns. On each of the four corners of the shoulder is an elephant head with a raised trunk and curved tusks. This vessel is elegant, beautifully decorated and excellently cast. Inside is a four-character inscription '*Gui Gu zuo lü*', meaning that Gui Gu commissioned this for a sacrificial ceremony. MA JINHONG

17

18

18 *Zhi* (wine vessel) made for His Majesty's Servant Shan

King Cheng's reign, Western Zhou (early 11th century BC)
Mouth 11.6 × 9.3 cm
Height 13.8 cm
Donated by Li Yinxuan and Qiu Hui.

This oblate ritual wine vessel, or *zhi*, is simply decorated with a band of interconnected birds and dragons with their heads turned backwards. This design is unique among ancient bronzes.

Although this *zhi* appears modest it contains an inscription inside of great historical value. This relates to the Western Zhou's campaign against rebels in the east led by Wu Geng, son of the defeated King Zhou of Shang. It took three years to quell the rebellion. This event is referred to in the inscription as '*cuo ke Shang*' (defeating the Shang). Several generals took part in this campaign, but historical documents record that the commander was the Duke of Zhou, a point confirmed by this short inscription. The owner of this vessel, His Majesty's Servant Shan, was a participant in the campaign and he was rewarded with ten strings of cowrie shells (a currency of the time) by the Duke of Zhou when the latter was camped at Chengqi. Shan commissioned the vessel to record this.

The inscription is only 22 characters, but it provides an invaluable confirmation of an important event at the start of the Zhou period and imparts great historical value to the vessel. MA JINHONG

19

20 *Fang ding* (food container) with inscription '*hou zhuo*'
King Zhao's reign, Western Zhou
(late 11th century BC)
Mouth 17.4 × 13.3 cm
Height 21.3 cm
Donated by Li Yinxuan and Qiu Hui.

19 *You* (wine vessel) with inscription '*gu fu ji*'
Early Western Zhou (11th century BC)
Diameter of mouth 15.7 cm
Height 33.2 cm

20

**21 *Fang ding* (food container)
with inscription '*de*'**
King Cheng's reign, Early Western Zhou
(early 11th century BC)
Mouth 18 × 14.2 cm
Height 24.4 cm

21

22

23

22 *Gui* (food container) with inscription *'jia'*

Early Western Zhou (11th century BC)
Diameter of mouth 22.5 cm
Height 29.8 cm
Donated by Tang Zugu and
Song Jingwen.

23 *Gui* (food container) made for E Shu

Early Western Zhou (11th century BC)
Diameter of mouth 18.1 cm
Height 18.5 cm

The *gui* is a ritual vessel for offerings of cooked millet, rice, sorghum and other staples. It appeared in the early Shang period, usually without handles, and became an important vessel although the form was only systemised after the mid-Western Zhou period. There were clear regulations about how many were allowed to be used according to the owners' rank. They were usually found in pairs and often also used together with *ding*.

This *gui* has a shallow belly and a stem foot resting on a high square pedestal. It has four animal-faced handles on the belly with hanging appendages or 'ears' and horns protruding above the rim. The form reflects a new style which appeared in the early Western Zhou period: a square bronze pedestal is cast together with the foot ring and with a three or four-handle *gui*. Large rectangular 'ears' on the handles become very popular. The *taotie* design on the stem foot shows the mouth, ears, eyes, eyebrows and two horns but omits the outline of the face. Each side of the square pedestal is decorated with a pair of facing phoenix in profile with long crests. All these relief decorations are set against a thunder-pattern background. There is a bell suspended from the base inside the stem foot and it still rings. Six characters are inscribed inside the vessel recording that it was made for E Shu. E was a kingdom in the Shang period but this piece was definitely made later than this. MA JINHONG

**24 Yan (food steamer) with
inscription 'mu gui'**
Early Western Zhou (11th century BC)
Diameter of mouth 31.3 cm
Height 50.2 cm

24

25

25 *You* (wine vessel) with inscription '*xiao*'
King Gong's reign, Western Zhou
(mid-10th century BC)
Mouth 13.2 × 9.7 cm
Height 24.3 cm
Donated by Xue Guisheng

26 *Hu* (wine flask) with inscription '*qi zhong*'
King Gong's reign, Western Zhou (mid-10th century BC)
Mouth 8.4 × 6.8 cm
Height 14.8 cm

27 *Fang yi* (wine vessel) with inscription '*shi ju*'
King Gong's reign, Western Zhou
(mid-10th century BC)
Mouth 9.8 × 7.6 cm
Height 16.4 cm
Donated by Ding Xierou

26

27

29 Da Ke *Ding* - Large *ding* (food container) made for Ke

King Xiao's reign, Western Zhou (late 10th century BC)
Diameter of mouth 75.6 cm
Height 93.1 cm
Weight 201.5 kg
Excavated at Ren Village, Famen Temple, Fufeng County, Shaanxi Province, 1890
Donated by Pan Dayu.

Ding are the most important of the ancient bronze ritual vessels and were in use for the longest period. They come in two basic shapes, round and square. Because the bases of some that have been excavated have burn marks it is hypothesized that their function was for cooking and holding cooked food.

This is a majestic and stately *ding* with a thick rim, broad body and three hoof-shaped feet. It has a stylized *taotie* design on the register under the rim and a bold rhythmical wave pattern around its heavy body. Above the hoof-shaped feet are *taotie* designs in deep relief. There is a long inscription of 290 characters inside the vessel whose content can be divided into two. The first is a eulogy from Ke to his grandfather, Shi Hua Fu. The second records the ceremony when King Zhou conferred upon Ke an important official post and items of his largess. This inscription is very important for throwing light on the social and economic system of the Western Zhou. It is written in large, simple and regulated characters with powerful strokes and is a masterpiece of Western Zhou calligraphy. Da Ke *Ding* is a treasure not only of the Shanghai Museum but also of the world.

The Da Ke *Ding* was excavated in the 16th year of the Guangxu reign period (1890). There were seven smaller *ding*s unearthed at same time which are called 'Xiao Ke *Ding*' (Small *ding*s of Ke). MA JINHONG

28 *Ling* (wine vessel) with inscription '*zhong yi fu*'

Mid Western Zhou
(late-11th century BC)
Diameter of mouth 15.5 cm
Height 44.2 cm
Excavated at Ren Village, Famen Temple, Fufeng County, Shaanxi Province, 1890.

28

29 >

30

32   *Hu* (wine flask) with dragon pattern
Late Western Zhou
(early 9th century – 771 BC)
Diameter of mouth 17.5 cm
Height 48.7 cm
Excavated at Qin Village, Baoji County,
Shaanxi Province, 1994.

30   *Gui* (food container) with inscription '*shi huai*'
King Xuan's reign (827 – 782 BC),
Western Zhou
Diameter of mouth 22.5 cm
Height 27 cm

31   *Xu* (food container) made for Fu, Duke of Jin
Late Western Zhou
(early 9th century – 771 BC)
Mouth 26.7 × 20 cm
Height 22.2 cm
Unearthed at Tomb 1, Beizhao Village,
Quwo County, Shanxi Province, 1992.

31

32 >

33

33 Yi (water container) made for Duke of Qi

Late Western Zhou (early 9th – 771 BC)

Length 48.1 cm

Height 24.7 cm

Donated by Shen Tongyue and others.

35 Fu (food container) with inscription 'shan she hu'

Early Spring and Autumn period

(770 BC – early 7th century)

Mouth 23.9 × 30 cm

Height 17.2 cm

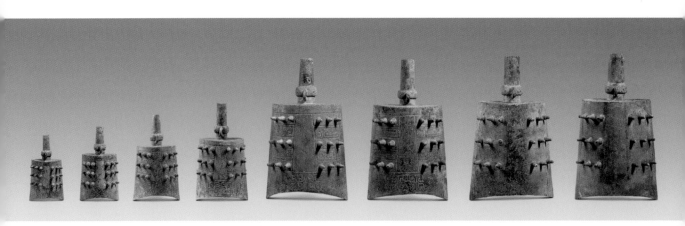

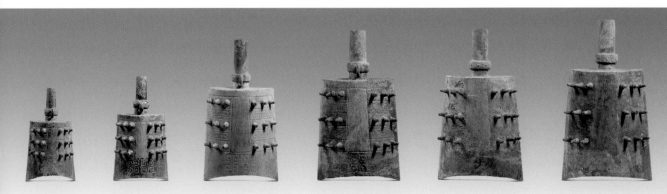

34

35

34 *Zhong* (bells) made for Su, Duke of Jin

King Li's reign, Western Zhou (mid-9th century BC)
Width 12.9 to 29.9 cm
Height 22.3 to 49 cm
Unearthed at Tomb 8, Beizhao Village, Quwo County,
Shanxi Province, 1992.

This set of musical bells comprises 16 pieces in total of which 14 are in
the Shanghai Museum and the other two are in the Shanxi Provincial
Institute of Archaeology. The set can be divided in two groups, each of
eight pieces. Their sound has been tested and proved that they ring in
harmony, indicating that the whole set belong together. A total of 355
characters are inscribed on the 16 bells, recording that in the 33rd year
of the reign of King Li, Su, Duke of Jin, and his army joined the battle led
by King Li against the Yi in the east. The Duke won many battles and
was repeatedly rewarded by King Li, hence he commissioned this set of
musical bells. The battle recorded on the bells is not recorded in any
other extant historical documents. Moreover, the inscriptions were
carved using metal chisels unlike previous inscriptions which were
cast. This is therefore the earliest example of chiselled inscriptions on
a Western Zhou bronze. MA JINHONG

34

36

36 *Pan* (water vessel) made for Zi Zhong Jiang

Early Spring and Autumn period (770 BC – early 7th century)
Diameter of mouth 45 cm
Height 18 cm
Donated by Ye Zhaofu.

Pan is a water bowl used to catch water after ritual washing at sacrificial ceremonies and banquets during the Shang and Zhou periods. *Pan* first appeared in the early Shang period and were popular from the late Shang to the Warring States period.

This is a heavy piece with stylized animal patterns on the outside. Two horned dragons are climbing up the sides with their heads just above the rim, as if looking into the water. The interior is decorated with many aquatic animals, both in relief and three-dimensional forms. In the centre is a three-dimensional bird encircled by five decorative rings. The first ring consists of two alternating sets of frogs and fish carved in shallow relief. The second is comprised of four three-dimensional fish. The third is made up of four alternating sets of frogs and tortoises in shallow relief. The fourth consists of four birds and four frogs all in three dimensions. The fifth is of fish carved in shallow relief. The most extraordinary feature is that all the three-dimensional animals can be swivelled as all are stuck onto vertical stems. This kind of decorative technique was completely novel at the time. When the vessel is full of water, the fish, tortoises, frogs and birds move in the water as if alive. There are three tigers holding up the base, depicted as if they are carrying heavy loads. This is also a novel design.

An inscription of 32 characters is cast inside the *pan*, recording that this was commissioned by a man for his wife, Zi Zhong Jiang. MA JINHONG

37

37 *Bo* (musical instrument) with inscription '*Qin Gong*'
Early Spring and Autumn period
(770 BC – early 7th century)
Width 24.5 cm
Height 38.2 cm

38 *Hu* (wine flask) with lotus-shaped lid and dragon pattern
Mid-Spring and Autumn period (early 7th century – early 6th century BC)
Diameter of the belly: 39.5 cm
Height 76.4 cm

38

39

39 Sacrificial animal *zun* (wine vessel)

Late Spring and Autumn period (early 6th century – 476 BC)
Length 58.7 cm
Height 33.7 cm
Excavated at Liyu Village, Hunyuan County, Shanxi Province, 1923.

This *zun* is modelled as a water buffalo. The belly of the buffalo is hollow and there
are three holes along its back. Inside the middle one is a removable pot-shaped
container which was used to hold wine. Hot water was poured into the hollow
belly to heat the wine. Many ancient Chinese bronze wine vessels were modelled
as animals. The nose ring shows that domesticated animals were used by this
period. The piece is finely decorated in shallow relief with *taotie* designs formed
from twisted dragons on the buffalo's head, neck, body and legs. There are tigers
and rhinoceros around the neck of the buffalo and on the pot-shaped container.
MA JINHONG

40

41

40 *Zun* **(wine vessel) with inlaid thorn pattern**
Late Spring and Autumn period (early 6th century – 476 BC)
Diameter of mouth 29.4 cm
Height 36.2 cm

41 *Hu* **(wine flask) with bird, animal and dragon design**
Late Spring and Autumn period (early 6th century – 476 BC)
Diameter of mouth 16.6 cm
Height 44.3 cm
Excavated at Liyu Village, Hunyuan County, Shanxi Province, 1923.

43 *Dou* (food container) with inlaid hunting scene

Late Spring and Autumn period (early 6th century – 476 BC)
Diameter of mouth 17.5 cm
Height 20.7 cm
Excavated at Liyu Village, Hunyuan County, Shanxi Province, 1923.

This is a characteristic *dou* comprised of a shallow bowl on a high stem foot ring with a bowl-shaped lid, also with a ring handle which acts as a foot when the lid is removed. Lids only became common in the Spring and Autumn period. The vessel's decoration, which is formed by inlaid copper, shows hunting scenes on the lid and the body. Fleeing animals, some already shot, are being chased by hunters with bows and arrows and knives. Decorations showing human figures also only appeared in the late Spring and Autumn period. The figures appear in banqueting scenes, in archery, harvesting mulberry leaves, hunting, wrestling, as soldiers besieging a city and in river battles. Ma Jinhong

42 *He* (wine vessel) with inscription Fu Chai, King of Wu

Late Spring and Autumn period (early 6th century – 476 BC)
Diameter of belly 24.9 cm
Height 27.8 cm
Donated by He Hongzhang.

42

43

43 detail

1.44 *Dou* (food container) with openwork carved dragon design
Late Spring and Autumn period
(early 6th century – 476 BC)
Diameter of mouth 23 cm
Height 26.7 cm

44

45

45 *Jian* (water vessel) made for Fu Chai, King of Wu

Late Spring and Autumn period (early 6th century – 476 BC)
Diameter of mouth 73 cm
Height 45 cm
Excavated in Hui County, Henan Province.

This *jian* has two looped handles with rings, decorated with two small creatures protruding just above the rim. Between them are two horned dragons climbing up the *jian* with the front claws and noses on the rim. The neck and belly of the vessel are decorated with interlaced dragon designs. That on the belly is in three registers, a narrow top band, a wider middle section and the lower comprised of triangular shapes. The design is complicated with the dragons tangled together. It was made by simple moulds being pressed against each other and then joined together. The imprint of the mould can still be seen on the vessel. Inside is an inscription of thirteen characters recording that Fu Chai, King of Wu, selected the best bronze and had this *jian* made for his own use.

According to the evidence from historical records and archaeological discoveries, *jian* had several uses: as a water vessel; a container for ice to keep food chilled; and as a mirror before bronze mirrors became popular. People also used it for washing. The form appeared in the middle of the Spring and Autumn period and became popular later in this period and during the subsequent Warring States period. They continue to be made during the Western Han. MA JINHONG

46 *Hu* **(wine flask) with inlaid images**
Early Warring States period
(475 – mid-4th century BC)
Diameter of belly 22.6 cm
Height 34.2 cm

47 *He* **(wine vessel) with inlaid bird and animal pattern in silver and gold**
Early Warring States period
(475 – mid-4th century BC)
Length 29.5 cm
Height 26.6 cm

46

47

49

48

48   Square *hu* (wine vessel) with inlaid geometric patterns
Late Warring States period (mid-4th century – 221 BC)
Mouth 12.9 × 12.9 cm
Height 52.4 cm

49   *Dui* (food container) with engraved cloud pattern
Late Warring States period (mid-4th century – 221 BC)
Diameter of mouth 16.5 cm
Height 28.1 cm

50   Square mirror with openwork inlaid geometric pattern
Warring States period
Width 18.5 cm

Bronze mirrors appeared as early as 2000 BC in China, developed during the Warring States and reached their peak in the Han to Tang. They continued to be used during the Song, Yuan, Ming and Qing periods and even in modern times.

Bronze mirrors from the Warring States are typically light and portable, with a string-patterned knob. The main decorative pattern is intricate and flowing and placed against a background of fine lines, creating a multi-layer effect. Special decorative techniques came into use during this period, such as openwork, inlaid gemstones, inlaid gold and silver and coloured designs.

This mirror is square and comprised of front and back sections which were cast separately. The thickness of the front is 0.2 cm. The back has a geometric openwork design. The border around the mirror was cast with the back and there is no decoration on the knob and its base. Its simplicity is in contrast to the elaborate and flamboyant designs created by the fine lines of inlaid red copper thread inlaid on a background formed by inlaid turquoise. There is a gold inlay star-shaped nail near each corner, and twelve more nails in a regular arrangement on the front and back. However, these nails are in different positions on each side indicating that they are not being used as rivets but have a purely decorative function. Between the nails are designs of dragons with heads turned back and created from gold and turquoise inlay. This is the most exquisite bronze mirror of this period discovered to date.
Ma Jinhong

50

Sculpture in China has a long and rich history. Archaeological discoveries include stone carved human and animal figures and pottery sculptures from pre-historic times. By the Qin and Han dynasties sculptural art is exemplified by the warriors of the First Emperor, the stone statues leading to General Huo Qubing's tomb and the pottery figures from the Han period, often termed the 'three paragons of Qin and Han sculpture'. Over the following centuries the introduction and dissemination of Buddhism resulted in Buddhist sculptures entering the mainstream of Chinese art. The Buddhist cave complexes at Dunhuang, Yungang, Longmen and Maijishan play a major part in Chinese sculptural history and this reached a peak in the Tang. There are numerous extant Buddhist statues, tomb statues and clay figurines from this period, many of them masterpieces. Great works continued to be produced at times during the Song, Ming and Qing periods. Regional sculptural art, such as wood and jade carving, also became popular and flourished during this later period.

The sculpture collection in the Shanghai Museum is filled with masterpieces of all types and periods. From tomb figurines and carved stones to Buddhist cave and temple sculptures, each has its own distinctive characteristics. The collection also contains representational pieces from all periods between the Warring States to the Qing. Many media are represented, including clay, pottery, jade, stone, copper and wood. There are relief carved bricks from the Han period, stone lions and other tomb statuary, painted wooden figurines from the Warring States, pottery figurines from the Western and Eastern Han periods, warriors from the Northern Wei to the Northern Qi periods, polychrome glazed horses from the Tang, and tomb figures of women, officials and animals from the Southern Tang. All these are exceptional works of art.

The Buddhist collection includes polychrome Dunhuang statues, a Buddha head from Longmen, a bodhisattva with crossed ankles, a head of a Heavenly King, a stele made for Wang Longsheng in the Northern Wei period, a stele made for Chen Huidang in 540, a stone Buddha of the Northern Qi, a gilded stone Buddha made for Monk Huiying in 546, a statue of Prince Siddhartha made for Daochang in 553, a bronze Amitābha Buddha from the Sui, Tang period stone Heavenly Kings, stone arhats from the Song, and wooden Buddhist sculptures from various temples dating to the Song and Jin periods. Li Bohua

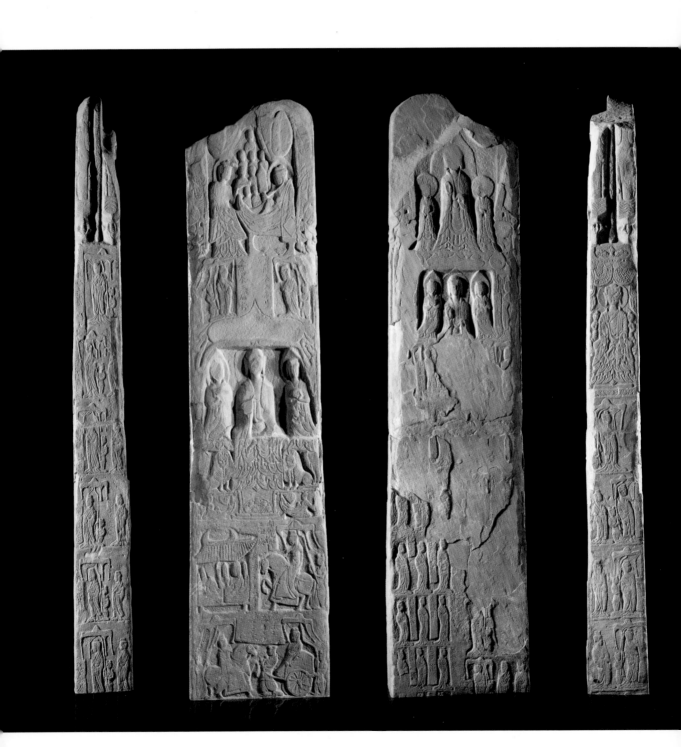

**51 Buddhist stele made
for Wang Longsheng
and others**
Northern Wei
Depth 20 cm
Width 50 cm
Height 233 cm

52 Gilded bronze Buddha
Northern Wei
Height 18 cm
Weight 850 g

**53 Buddhist stele made for
Chen Huidang and others**
6th year of the Datong reign period,
Western Wei (540)
Depth 14.5 cm
Width 58 cm
Height 90.5 cm

53

52

54

55

56

54 Stone statue of Šākyamuni Buddha

Northern Qi
Width 88 cm, Height 164 cm
Base 62 × 45 cm

55 Gold painted stone statue of Šākyamuni Buddha made for the monk Huiying

1st year of the Zhongdatong reign period, Liang (546)
Pedestal 9 × 17.8 cm, Height 34.2 cm
Weight 6750 g
Donated by Gu Yan.

This statue is carved in high relief against an arch-shaped screen which rises to a slight point and extends on either side slightly beyond the pedestal at the bottom. The central figure of Šākyamuni Buddha sitting in the lotus position on the pedestal is flanked by two disciples, Ānanda and Kāśyāpa, and two bodhisattvas. The disciples are incised on the screen, looking up at the Buddha. The attendant bodhisattvas standing on lotus pedestals are in high relief both wearing high crowns and smiling. An incense burner and a pair of lively guardian lions are carved on the central pedestal. There is a scene inscribed at the top of the screen with the title, 'Šākyamuni's first sermon'. This is a famous event in the historical Buddha's life when, following his enlightenment, he preached to his disciples in the Deer Park at Sarnath near Benares. The scene is arranged with Buddha and two bodhisattvas at the top and his disciples below. The incised patterns represent the landscape of mountain, rocks and clouds. In many respects the scene resembles a Chinese painting which indicates the influence of Chinese painting on Buddhist art at this time.

    On the back is a 54-character vow beginning with the date: 'In the first year of Zhongdatong reign of the Liang period...' (546). Only a few portable statues survive from the Southern Dynasties and this reign period in the Liang only lasted one year. This dated votive statue is thus extremely rare and key to the study of Southern Dynasties' Buddhist sculpture. LI BOHUA

56 Statue of Prince Siddhartha made for Daochang

4th year of the Tianbao reign period, Northern Qi (553)
Depth 19.8 cm
Width 27.5 cm. Height 52 cm

57 Thousand-Buddha Stele

Northern Zhou
Depth 17 cm
Width 81 cm, Height 171 cm

57

58

58 Amitābha grouping in bronze

Sui
Table 23.8 × 32.8 cm
Height 37.6 cm

This rectangular altar table shows Amitābha, with two bodhisattvas,
two donors and two guardian lions. There are empty sockets on either
side of Amitābha's lotus seat for figures of two disciples, now lost.

Amitābha sits cross-legged on the lotus seat, with his robe revealing
his right shoulder. His peach-shaped mandorla is decorated with a
border of flame patterns enclosing an openwork banyan tree with
seven small Buddhas on its branches. The attendant bodhisattvas are
turned towards Amitābha. They both have exquisitely carved
openwork floral halos and their crowns have a small Buddha in the
centre. The bodhisattva on the Buddha's left has a pearl in his right
hand while his left hand holds his flowing silk sash. The other
bodhisattva holds a flower in his left hand and his sash in his right. Both
bodhisattvas wear long necklaces of gems which hang down to their
knees. The two small figures of the donors, a man and a woman, are
showing their respect to Amitābha. This sculpture is exquisitely cast,
reflecting the extraordinary technical skills of the Sui period. LI BOHUA

59

60

59 Stone Avalokiteśvara

Sui
Width 35 cm
Height 150 cm
Weight 125 kg

60 Stone Mahāsthāmaprāpta

Sui
Width 42 cm
Height 148 cm
Weight 137.5 kg

This pair of stone statues of Avalokiteśvara and
Mahāsthāmaprāpta is the only one found from this period
and an outstanding example of Sui sculpture. Avalokiteśvara
wears a floral crown with a small Amitābha Buddha. His
modelling and decoration are exquisite. Mahāsthāmaprāpta,
the other attending bodhisattva of Amitābha, also wears a
crown and beads. This grouping of these two with Amitābha
Buddha is known as 'The venerable triad of Amitābha'.
LI BOHUA

61 Stone bodhisattva
Tang
Height c. 209 cm

62 Gilded bronze Buddha
Tang
Height 19.4 cm
Weight 1080 g

62

61

64

63

63 Wooden head of Kāśyāpa
Tang
Height 100 cm

64 Gilded bronze bodhisattva
Tang
Height 29.7 cm
Weight 2120 g

65

65 Gilded bronze bodhisattva
Liao
Height 46.9 cm
Weight 6060 g

66 Stone Heavenly King
Song
Height 186 cm

66

67 Stone statue of Kāśyāpa
Song
Height 169 cm

68 Stone statue of Ānanda
Song
Height 172 cm

67

68

69   Gilded and painted wooden bodhisattva
Jin
Height 130 cm

70   Gilded bronze statue of Uṣṇīṣavijaya
Qing
Depth 14.4 cm
Width 21 cm
Height 26.2 cm
Weight 5600 g

70

69 >

3

Earthenware and Stoneware

There are many forms of Chinese pottery in the Shanghai Museum. They range from Neolithic hand-made to wheel-made earthenware, from red, grey and black pottery to painted pots with vibrant decorations. These pieces are of great value both as display pieces and as research objects. The Museum's collection of painted pottery is especially rich in its variety and quality. Pieces excavated from sites of the Songze and the Liangzhu cultures close to Shanghai represent the highest standard of Neolithic earthenware in this area. During the Shang and Zhou periods pottery production was no longer so dominant. However, the Shanghai Museum still has some outstanding pieces, such as white wares and pottery with stamped patterns.

The collection from the Han period contains both glazed and unglazed wares each with its own characteristics. The unglazed pieces include many beautifully fashioned figurines. The lead glazed earthenware was fired at low temperatures and includes fine examples of mortuary pieces, such as yellow and green dogs and ducks which have taken on a silvery sheen owing to the glaze degrading in the tomb. The museum is also rich in its collection of polychrome lead glazed Tang pottery fired at low temperatures (commonly known as 'Tang Sancai' – 'Tang Three-Coloured Wares'). This collection showcases the skills needed to make the objects, which include horses, camels, civil servants, soldiers, women, tomb guardians and many utensils.

Production of stoneware declined from the late Tang period onwards as porcelain gradually became dominant in Chinese ceramics. During the Ming and Qing periods, Jingdezhen porcelain monopolised the market, but some provincial centres became well known and produced important pieces. These included purple stoneware from Yixing, Jiangsu Province, and various glazed stoneware from Shiwan, Guangdong Province. A great many pots were made by Yixing craftsmen during the Qing. LU MINGHUA

Continued overleaf

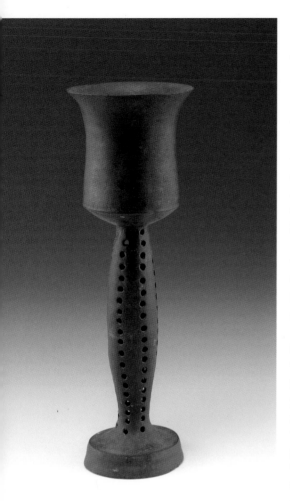

71

71 Openwork carved black earthenware *dou*

Late Dawenkou Culture, Neolithic
(2800 – 2400 BC)
Diameter of mouth 7.25 cm
Diameter of base 6.05 cm
Height 17.5 cm

This high-stemmed slender cup – or *dou* — has a wheel finished rim, a cylindrical body and a stem with a centre bulge. There is a line of round holes arranged evenly on the top part of the stem. This kind of openwork carving, while adding to the beauty, also reduces the weight of the object without affecting its balance. The foot ring is also hollow. The body of the cup is very thin, so it is also called 'egg-shell' pottery, and the ability to make this indicates the advancement in technology of the time, most especially the use of a wheel. ZHANG DONG

Porcelain

Porcelain is one of China's great inventions. Porcelain firing has a long history in China, where its technology has become very complex. Most items of porcelain in the Shanghai Museum have been handed down through generations and show the whole of porcelain's development. It is therefore a very influential collection both inside and outside China. It includes pieces which preceded porcelain, such as high-fired earthenware from the Han, glazed stoneware of the Six Dynasties and Sui periods, and Tang celadon – green or brown-glazed stoneware. The collection contains many masterpieces of green Yue wares from Zhejiang, and white Xing wares from northern China.

The porcelain industry thrived in the Song period. There were five famous kilns and numerous smaller local kilns. Many masterpieces were produced and the Museum's collection of Song and Jin porcelain reflects this. It would not be extravagant to say that the collection provides a microcosm of this flourishing period.

Porcelain from the Jingdezhen kilns started to become dominant from the Yuan. Many successful firing techniques were developed there, such as blue and white, underglazed red, over glazing, and monochromes. Jingdezhen soon became the main porcelain production centre in China and the Museum has a large and varied collection, all exquisitely made and including some very rare pieces. There are outstanding blue and white and added colour Yuan wares, and porcelain from the Ming imperial kilns during the Hongwu, Yongle, Xuande, Chenghua reign periods and from the late Ming. Wonderful pieces representing the characteristics of their times also appear among porcelains of the Kangxi, Yongzheng and Qianlong reign periods of the Qing dynasty. Jingdezhen porcelain forms the single most important part of the Museum's collection.

Other areas also made contributions to porcelain production at this time. The collection reflects this in its pieces of *blanc de chine* from Dehua in Fujian, polychrome glazes from Zhangzhou and celadon from Longquan in Zhejiang. LU MINGHUA

72

73

72 Painted earthenware *hu* (wine flask) with string pattern

Majiayao Culture, Neolithic
(3300 – 2900 BC)
Diameter of mouth 9 cm
Diameter of base 11 cm
Height 29 cm

73 Red earthenware *gui* (food container)

Neolithic period (6500-1700 BC)
Height 23.8 cm
Donated by Xu Menghua.

74 Openwork carving black earthenware *guan* with a high stem and lid

Liangzhou Culture, Neolithic
(2310 – 1810 BC)
Diameter of mouth 7.2 cm
Diameter of base 9.2 cm
Height 20.5 cm

75

75 Green glazed *zun* (wine vessel) with string pattern

Shang period (c. 1500 – 1050 BC)
Diameter of mouth 19.65 cm
Diameter of base 9.9 cm
Diameter of belly 11.5 cm
Height 18 cm

This piece has a wheel finished mouth and a yellowish-green glaze which is thinly and evenly applied over the whole of the light grey body except for the base. The overall decoration consists of eight groups of string patterns, with an impressed square pattern at the bottom. This Shang glazed ware was fired at a higher temperature than previous wares and therefore can be seen as an early step in the long development to the higher fired porcelains and celadon wares. Like many of the ceramics from this period, the shape is similar to the bronze vessels. It is a fine example of Shang glazed ware.
ZHANG DONG

76 Green glazed *ding* (food container) with animal head

Warring States
Diameter 13.6 cm
Height 14.9 cm

76

77 Yellow glazed dog
Eastern Han
Height 48.5 cm

78

78 Green glazed talisman
Western Jin
Length 19.9 cm
Height 13.4 cm

79 Black glazed flask with four rings and wide mouth, Deqing ware
Eastern Jin
Diameter of mouth 4 cm
Diameter of belly 18.8 cm
Diameter of base 11.4 cm
Height 24.9 cm

79

80

80   Green glazed *hu* (wine flask) with lotus petal pattern
Northern Dynasties
Diameter of mouth 10.5 cm
Diameter of base 10.5 cm
Height 19.9 cm

81   Polychrome glazed earthenware camel
Sui
Length 50.9 cm
Height 47.3 cm

82   Polychrome glazed earthenware horse
Tang
Length 73 cm
Height 66 cm

81

82 >

83

84

83 Yue ware green glazed begonia-shaped bowl

Tang
Diameter of mouth 23.3 × 32.2 cm
Diameter of base 11.4 cm
Height 10.8 cm

This oval bowl has four indentations on the rim and resembles a begonia flower in its shape. Like many Yue wares, the form is modelled on Sassanian silver wares, popular in China at the time. A round bowl was made first then placed over a begonia-shaped mould to create the oval shape. The foot was added on later and hand finished. There are marks of burnt clay inside the bowl and on its base, indicating that when this bowl was fired a smaller vessel was placed inside it and, in turn, it was placed inside a larger vessel, the method of 'stacked firing'. The glaze, which covers the piece, is a lustrous jade-like green. This is an outstanding piece of Tang period Yue ware. Zhang Dhong

84 Ru ware dish

Northern Song
Diameter of mouth 17.1 cm
Diameter of base 9.1 cm
Height 2.9 cm

This shallow dish has a wheel finished rim and a slightly flared base, inside which are five spur marks from firing. The glaze, which covers the piece, is an opaque sky blue and cracked, typical of these wares and called 'cracked ice pattern' in historical documents. The body is a fine grained yellow-grey and is commonly known as 'incense ash body'. The shape is simple yet elegant. Using spurs to support the piece on a stand during firing enabled it to be glazed both inside and out, another characteristic of Ru ware. Zhang Dong

85

85 Jingdezhen *qingbai* glazed ewer and bowl

Northern Song
Height (altogether) 26.1 cm

86 Ge ware five-footed basin
Song
Diameter of mouth 18.8 cm
Height 9.2 cm

87 Yaozhou ware green glazed _meiping_ with engraved peony design
Northern Song
Diameter of mouth 7.5 cm
Diameter of base 11 cm
Height 48.4 cm

88 Ding ware white glazed dish with impressed cloud and dragon design
Jin
Diameter of mouth 23.15 cm
Diameter of base 10.7 cm
Height 4.9 cm

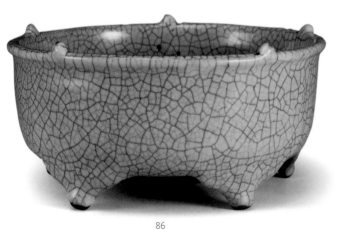

86

87

89

88

89 Yaozhou ware tiger-shaped pillow with black and white flower and bird design
2nd year of Dading reign period, Jin
(1162)
Length 19.5 cm
Width 39.6 cm
Height 12.8 cm

90

90   Jizhou ware black glazed wine cup with leaf decoration (leaf *temmoku*)
Song
Diameter of mouth 10.7 cm
Diameter of base 3 cm
Height 4.6 cm

91   Huairen ware bowl with oil-spot glaze
Jin
Diameter of mouth 21 cm
Diameter of base 6.8 cm
Height 9.8 cm

92   Guan ware two-eared censer
Southern Song
Diameter of mouth 11 cm
Diameter of base 8.5 cm
Height 8.4 cm
Donated by Zhang Xuejing.

91

92

93

93 Chifeng ware *guan* with black and white engraved peony design
Liao
Diameter of mouth 23.9 cm
Diameter of base 14.3 cm
Height 29.9 cm

94   Longquan ware or southern celadon jar with dragon relief lid
Southern Song
Diameter of mouth 6.5 cm
Diameter of base 6.65 cm
Height 22.6 cm

95   Jun ware sky-blue glazed tripod censer with red splashes and appliqué ears
Yuan
Diameter of mouth 23.9 cm
Height (including handles) 35.8 cm

96   *Qingbai* glazed Buddha
Yuan
Height 41.3 cm

94

96 >

95

97

98

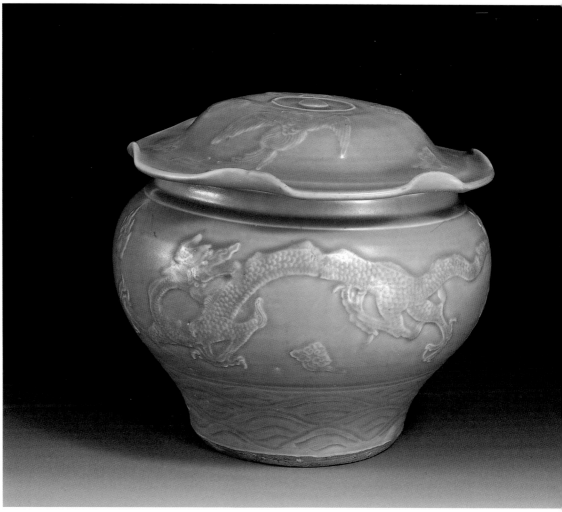

99

97 Blue and white jar with peony design

Yuan

Diameter of mouth 20.7 cm

Diameter of base 18.6 cm

Height 27.5 cm

98 Jingdezhen *qingbai* glazed dish with embossed decorations and added colour

Yuan

Diameter of mouth 16.1 cm

Diameter of base 5.5 cm

Height 4.3 cm

99 Longquan ware celadon jar and lid with dragon design

Yuan

Diameter of mouth 24.8 cm

Diameter of base 18 cm

Height 28.6 cm

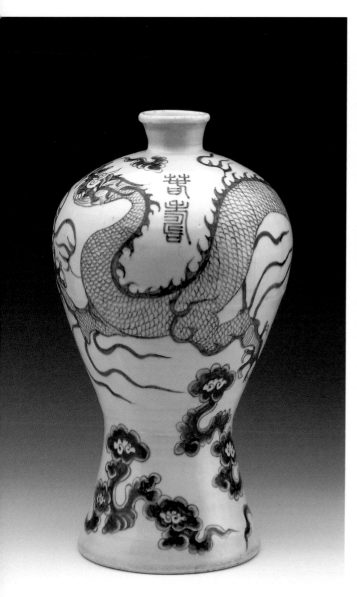

100

101

100 Blue and white cloud and dragon design vase with characters 'spring longevity'
Hongwu reign period, Ming
Diameter of mouth 10.9 cm
Diameter of base 14.3 cm
Height 45.5 cm

101 Underglaze copper red vase with two ear handles and cloud and dragon design
Hongwu reign period, Ming
Diameter of mouth 10.9 cm
Diameter of base 14.3 cm
Height 45.5 cm

This large vase has a thick and heavy body, with a design of a fierce and sturdy three-clawed dragon decorating the belly. The copper red glaze is a brownish colour due to poor reduction or too thin a glaze. Underglaze copper red porcelains were common during the Hongwu reign period and the technique and glaze became refined during the early fifteenth century. However, the style then went into a decline and only recovered at the beginning of the Qing in the seventeenth century. PENG TAO

102

---

102   Blue and white oblate flask with camellia design
Yongle reign period, Ming
Diameter of base 7.6 × 10.1 cm
Diameter of mouth 3.1 cm
Height 24.9 cm

This type of oblate flask is commonly known as 'embracing the moon flask'
or 'precious moon flask'. Its body is light and thin and the shape was
adopted from Islamic silverware. During this time there was an increase in
trade from China to Western Asia and elsewhere. The main motif is the
camellia spray on either side of the belly. The composition is well-balanced,
with a good sense of space. The underglaze painting is an intense blue,
with slight black areas where it has broken through the glaze to oxidise.
The white glaze has a tint of blue and some undulation usually referred to
as 'orange peel'. All these are typical of early fifteenth century wares.
PENG TAO

103

104

103   Red glazed *anhua* (secret decoration) dish
Yongle reign period, Ming
Diameter of mouth 14.8 cm
Diameter of base 8.9 cm
Height 3.5 cm

104   White glazed 'monk's hat' jug
Yongle reign period, Ming
Diameter of mouth 11.5 cm
Diameter of base 7.3 cm
Height 19.8 cm

105   *Zun* (wine vessel) with white dragon reserved on a blue ground
Xuande reign period, Ming
Diameter of mouth 16 cm
Diameter of base 11.9 cm
Height 14 cm

106   Underglaze red stem bowl decorated with three fish
Xuande reign period, Ming
Diameter of mouth 9.9 cm
Diameter of base 4.5 cm
Height 8.8 cm

107   Dish with red glazed design of floral sprays on a white ground
Xuande reign period, Ming
Diameter of mouth 38.5 cm
Diameter of base 28.2 cm
Height 6.6 cm

105

106

107

108

108   Blue and white *guan* jar with illustrations of the four accomplishments: music, chess, calligraphy and painting

Xuande reign period, Ming
Diameter of mouth 22.1 cm
Diameter of base 21.8 cm
Height 34.4 cm
Donated by Hu Huichun and Wang Huayun.

The four illustrations are depicted inside landscapes of caves, rocks, pines, bamboos and clouds in a rich blue. The human figures are all female showing clear facial features. Such figurative scenes are rare on Xuande period porcelains. PENG TAO

109   Jingdezhen blue and white bowl with dragon design

Chenghua reign period, Ming
Diameter of mouth 17 cm
Diameter of base 7.4 cm
Height 9 cm

Blue and white porcelain reached a peak in the early fifteenth century, but flourished later in the century during the Chenghua reign period. Chenghua porcelain cannot compete with the earlier ware in quantity and variety, but it has a thinner and lighter porcelain body, smoother glazing and a perfected firing technique.

This dish is a typical blue and white ware from the imperial kiln with a pure glossy glaze. Blue and white wares had previously used imported cobalt blue known as *sulimānī* but in this period the pigment was mined in China, from Leping, Jiangxi Province. This was paler, easier to control and gave a more even colour. The dragon on the bowl is like a traditional dragon in its lively characterisation but lacking ferocity and power. It was a very popular motif during this period. ZHOU LILLI

110 Peacock blue enamel bowl with blue and white lotus and fish design
Chenghua reign period, Ming
Diameter of mouth 23.5 cm
Diameter of base 15.15 cm
Height 5.05 cm

111

111   Enamelled *doucai* vase
Chenghua reign period, Ming
Height 18.1 cm

112   Yellow glazed dish
Hongzhi reign period, Ming (1487–1505)
Diameter of mouth 21.5 cm
Diameter of base 13.1 cm
Height 4.4 cm

**113   Blue and yellow enamelled
large dish with dragon design**
Jiajing reign period, Ming
Diameter of mouth 79 cm
Diameter of base 54.5 cm
Height 10.5 cm
Donated by Hu Huichun & Wang
Huayun.

112

113

114

115

114　Polychrome *wucai* enamelled *guan* jar with dragon design

Jiajing reign period, Ming
Diameter of mouth 21.8 cm
Diameter of base 18.8 cm
Height 37.4 cm

115　Polychrome *wucai* enamelled brush box

Wanli reign period, Ming
Height with lid 8.9 cm
Length 29.9 cm

116　Blue and white vase with landscape painting

Chongzhen reign period, Ming
Diameter of mouth 13.2 cm
Diameter of base 13.7 cm
Height 47.3 cm

117

117 Blue and white figurine seated on an animal and blowing a shell
Wanli reign period, Ming
Height 26.4 cm

118 Dehua *blanc de chine* figure of Avalokiteśvara with mark of He Chaozong, Dehua ware
Ming
Height 48 cm

118 >

119

119 Enamelled jar with fish and seaweed design

Kangxi reign period, Qing
Diameter of mouth 6.4 cm
Diameter of base 6 cm
Height 22.1 cm

120 Enamelled bowl with peony design

Kangxi reign period, Qing
Diameter of mouth 14.7 cm
Diameter of base 6.7 cm
Height 7.5 cm

121 Enamelled *doucai* dish with design of birds worshipping a phoenix

Kangxi reign period, Qing
Diameter of mouth 55.4 cm
Diameter of base 32.1 cm
Height 9.6 cm

120

121

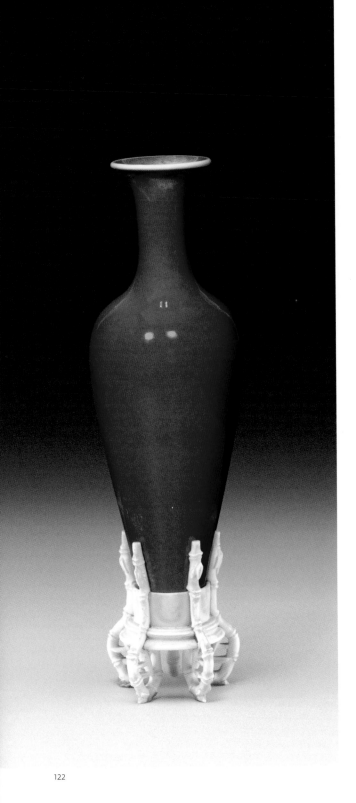

122

123 Jingdezhen *famille rose* vase with peach and bat design

Yongzheng reign period, Qing
Diameter of mouth 10 cm
Diameter of base 12.5 cm
Height 39.5 cm
Donated by Zhang Yongzhen.

From the end of the Kangxi reign period a rose-coloured enamel started to be used in Chinese porcelain production. Called *famille rose* the technique replaced other polychrome enamels and became the mainstream overglaze colouring during the Qing. The technique was perfected in the Yongzheng and Qianlong reign periods. Those from the Yongzheng period were in many shapes, with rich, luxurious colours, while the Qianlong period wares are characterised by finer bodies, prettier shapes and more subtle colours and elegant designs.

The vase is decorated with a peach and bats design in exquisite *famille rose*. The words for 'bat' and 'peach' are homonymous with those for 'good luck' and 'longevity' in Chinese. These types of motif usually appear on dishes and are rarely seen on vases. ZHOU LILI

122 Ladybird red glazed jar

Kangxi reign period, Qing
Diameter of mouth 3.4 cm
Diameter of base 2 cm
Height 15.3 cm

123

123

124

125

126

124 Celadon jar with cloud and dragon design
Yongzheng reign period, Qing
Diameter of mouth 40.6 cm
Diameter of base 32 cm
Height 45.5 cm

125 Enamelled bowl with design of black bamboo
Yongzheng reign period, Qing
Diameter of mouth 16.1 cm
Diameter of base 4 cm
Height 7.58 cm

126 Pomegranate shaped wine vessel in Ge ware style
Yongzheng reign period, Qing
Diameter of mouth 7.6 cm
Height 16.8 cm

127 Blue and white oblate vessel with longevity motif and dragon shaped handles
Qianlong reign period, Qing
Base 17.8 × 12 cm
Diameter of mouth 8 cm
Height 49.4 cm

127

128 **Celadon bowl and lid with** *anhua* **and gilt decorations, with a tea-dust glaze pedestal**

Qianlong reign period, Qing

Diameter of mouth 12.6 cm

Diameter of base: 9.3 cm

Height (with lid) 10.9 cm

129 **Flambé glaze vase**

Qianlong reign period, Qing

Diameter of mouth 11.2 cm

Diameter of base 9 cm

Height 19.5 cm

128

129

130

131

130 Enamelled vase with bamboo, chrysanthemum and quails

Qianlong reign period, Qing
Diameter of mouth 5.55 cm
Diameter of base 6.2 cm
Height 19.15 cm

The enamelled porcelains of the Kangxi, Yongzheng and Qianlong reign periods each show their own characteristics. The Kangxi wares still refer to enamelled metalwork in their colouring and decoration. Yongzheng wares make the break from this and combine traditional Chinese decorations with poetry, calligraphy, paintings and seals. Qianlong enamels added western painting techniques. The compositions and decorations become more elaborate and the shapes more diverse showing advances in enamel production techniques.

The bamboo, chrysanthemum and quail decoration on this vase is a motif meaning a long and peaceful reign, and shows the hand of an imperial artist. The work is exquisite and the details are painted with meticulous care. The base is inscribed with four characters, 'made in the Qianlong reign', in *zhuan* or seal script enclosed in a double blue rectangle. This is a typical porcelain of the Qing imperial court. ZHUO LILI

131 Gold, *kinrande*, peach decorated vase on blue

Qianlong reign period, Qing
Diameter of mouth 9.35 cm
Diameter of base 15 cm
Height 23.35 cm

132

132 Vase with red lotus sprays on a white ground
Qianlong reign period, Qing
Diameter of mouth 5 cm
Diameter of base 5.7 cm
Height 21 cm

133 Vase with red floral spray and dragon design
Qianlong reign period, Qing
Diameter of mouth 12.5 cm
Diameter of belly 21 cm
Diameter of base 13.4 cm
Height 37.3 cm

133>

134

134 Celadon oblate vase with carved cloud and bird design

Qianlong reign period, Qing
Diameter of mouth 9.8 × 6.4 cm
Length of base 11.9 cm
Width of base 9.1 cm
Height 36.9 cm

135 Yellow glazed brush pot with mark of Chen Guozhi

Daoguang reign period, Qing
Diameter of mouth 15.6 cm
Diameter of base 14.7 cm
Height 13.9 cm

136 Yixing teapot with mark of Mansheng

Jiaqing reign period, Qing
Diameter of mouth 6 cm
Diameter of belly 11.9 cm
Height 18.35 cm
Donated by Tang Yun.

135

136

4

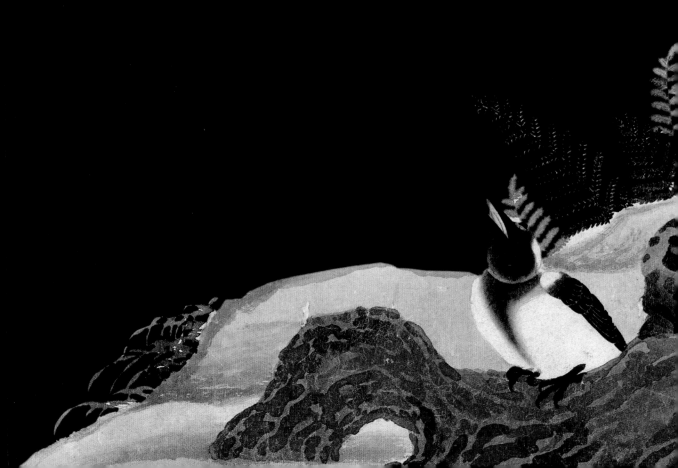

The painting collection of the Shanghai Museum is reputed to comprise 'half the total collection of Southern China'. It is one of the most important of all the Chinese museum collections of paintings, notable for several reasons. First, it contains many masterpieces from different periods, all of them significant in the history of Chinese art. For example, *Hermits*, by Sun Wei of the late Tang, is one of the very few authentic masterpieces from the Tang Dynasty and provides important research material for Tang figurative painting. Other outstanding examples include *Carts and Waterwheels* from the Five Dynasties, *Crows on Willows and Wild Geese in Reeds* by Zhao Jie of the Northern Song, *Retreat in the Qingbian Mountains* by Wang Meng of the Yuan. Secondly, the collection contains the only extant copies of many works, such as the *Landscape after a Poem by Du Fu* by Zhao Kui of the Southern Song, which fills a gap in the history of Chinese painting. Thirdly, the Ming and Qing painting collection represents a comprehensive history and development of this period. Shanghai Museum has more works than any other Chinese museum of the so-called 'The Ming Masters', 'The Songjiang School of Painting', 'The Four Wangs of the Qing' and Wu Yun's, 'Four Buddhist Masters'.

Over the last few years the Shanghai Museum has held many large-scale special exhibitions on ancient Chinese painting and calligraphy, including 'National Treasures of Calligraphy and Painting from the Jin, Tang, Song and Yuan Dynasties'; 'Rare Masterpieces of Painting and Calligraphy'. These exhibitions aroused great media interest and attracted scholars and visitors from around the world. The painting and calligraphy exhibition hall has frequently changing exhibits of treasures from the collection and allow visitors the best opportunity to appreciate these treasures and carry out research. LI LAN

137

137

137 Hermits
Sun Wei (active late 9th century)
Tang
Handscroll, ink and colour on silk
Length 45.3 cm, Width 169.1 cm

Sun Wei was a native of Kuaiji (present-day Shaoxing, Zhejiang Province) who became a painter for the Tang court. He was said to be accomplished in painting several traditional subjects, including figure painting, landscapes with pines and rocks, dragons with water, and Buddhist images. This is his only extant work.

This painting itself bears neither a painter's seal nor signature, but at the beginning is the note, '*Sun Wei Gao Yi Tu*' (*Hermits* by Sun Wei), written in the unique thin regular script of the Song emperor, Huizong (r. 1100–25). Research has proved that this painting is a section of *The Seven Sages of the Bamboo Grove*, referring to a common subject depicting seven semi-historical scholars of the Wei-Jin period who renounced political life. Four of the seven sages are seen in this section: Shandao, Wang Rong, Liu Ling and Ruan Ji. They sit on brightly coloured carpets, with four attendants and trees and rocks around them. All the figures are vividly depicted. Sharp lines are combined with soft strokes and the colour of the painting is rich and elegant. The seals are from Song imperial court, and include 'Yushu' (The Emperor's Hand) and 'Xuanhe' (Xuanhe reign period (1119-26). Li Lan

138

138 Travelling among Mountains and Streams
Zhu Cheng (10th century)
Five Dynasties
Album, ink and colour on silk
Height 26 cm, Width 24.8 cm

139

140   Crows on Willows and Wild Geese in Reeds

Zhao Ji (1082 – 1135)
Northern Song
Handscroll, ink and colour on silk
Height 34 cm, Width 223.2 cm

Zhao Ji was the name of the Northern Song emperor Hongzong (r.1101–1126), a native of Zhuo County (present-day Hebei Province). During his twenty-five year reign he devoted himself to painting and calligraphy more than to state affairs.

The first half of the painting shows an old willow tree on a slope, with four white-headed crows resting on the branches and among the roots, looking as if they are in conversation. The second half shows four wild geese, all with different expressions. The painting is ink wash with a thin layer of colour.

The signature reads 'One Under Heaven', a mark of this emperor. The seals include 'Yushu' (The Emperor's Hand) and 'Zichendian Yushu bao' (Treasure of the Emperor's Hand from the Purple Palace (i.e. the Court)).
LI LAN

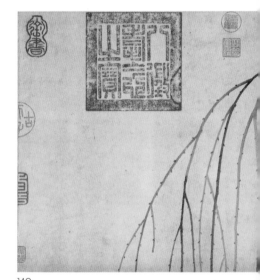

140

140

139 Misty River and Layered Peaks
Wang Shen (1036 – after 1093)
Nothern Song
Handscroll, ink and colour on silk
Height 45.2 cm, Width 166 cm

141

142

143 detail

141 A Bird on a Snowy Tree in Winter
Li Di (12th century)
Southern Song
Hanging scroll, ink and colour on silk
Height 115.2 cm, Width 52.8 cm

142 Bamboo and Sparrows

Wu Bing (active 1190–94)
Southern Song
Album, ink and colour on silk
Height 25 cm, Width 25 cm

143 Eight Eminent Monks

Liang Kai (active early 13th century)
Southern Song
Handscroll, ink and colour on silk
Height 26.6 cm, Width 64.1 cm

Liang Kai was from Dongping (present day Shandong Province), but mainly lived in Qiantang (present-day Hangzhou), the centre of the Imperial Painting Academy. He was appointed as a Painter-in-Attendance but later left to take up residence in a Buddhist temple and changed his repertoire from traditional subjects to Chan (Zen) paintings.

This painting comprises eight sections telling the stories of the eight eminent monks or Patriarchs of Chan Buddhism. They are depicted as individuals in different settings. In the first section, Bodhidharma, the Buddhist monk who brought Chan to China the 520s, is shown in a tranquil valley. Dressed in a red robe, he is sitting on a rock racing a wall in meditation with a serene and serious expression. This refers to the nine years he is said to have spent in meditation at Shaolin Monastery.

(cont'd)

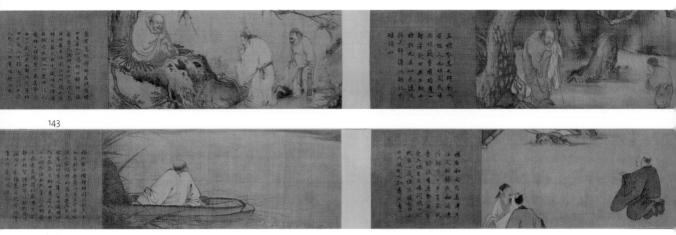

143

143

Shenguang, his disciple and the Second Patriarch of Chan, stands behind him. In contrast to the still human figures, the rocks are full of vigour, painted in a style know as axe-cut strokes. This is one of the most outstanding of Liang Kai's extant works. His signature appears on sections 2, 3, 5 and 8. LI LAN

143

143

143

143 Eight Eminent Monks
Liang Kai (active early 13th century)
Southern Song
Handscroll, ink and colour on silk
Height 26.6 cm, Width 64.1 cm

144

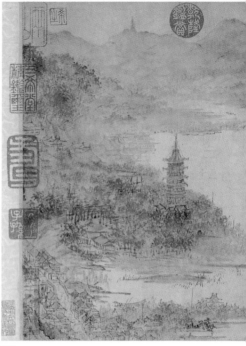

145

144 Walking in the Wilderness with a Stick

Ma Lin (12th–13th century)
Southern Song
Album, ink and colour on silk
Height 23.3 cm, Width 23.7 cm

145 Western Lake

Unknown
Southern Song
Handscroll, ink on paper
Height 27 cm, Width 80.7 cm

146 Poppy

Unknown
Southern Song
Album, ink and colour on silk
Height 25.5 cm, Width 26.2 cm

146

147

148

148 Retreat on Fuyu Mountain

Qian Xuan (c.1235–after 1299)
Yuan
Handscroll, ink and colour on paper
Length 29.6 cm, Width 98.7 cm

Qian Xuan was a painter of late Song/early Yuan period, who carried the style name Shunju and the literary name Yutan. He was a native of Wuxing (present-day Huzhou, Zhejiang Province). He specialised in human figures, flowers and birds, vegetables and fruits, and landscape paintings.

This painting is also called *Retreat in the Cloudy Mountains* and depicts the scenery of Fuyu Mountain in Zhachuan, where Qian Xuan lived in retreat. The mountain scenery shows deep valleys and gorges with misty floating clouds. There is a village half hidden by the trees and an old man walking slowly on the bridge. It is a peaceful, dreamlike scene. The rocks are outlined with fine brush strokes and shaded with ink wash. Light colours are applied on the trees and grass.

This is an outstanding example of Qian Xuan's art. Many eminent figures from the Yuan and Ming periods have written poems and inscriptions on the painting and there are also over three hundred seals of the various Yuan, Ming and Qing collectors. Lı Lan

147 Autumn Water with Birds

Ren Renfa (1255–1327)
Yuan
Hanging scroll, ink and colour on silk
Height 114.3 cm, Width 57.2 cm

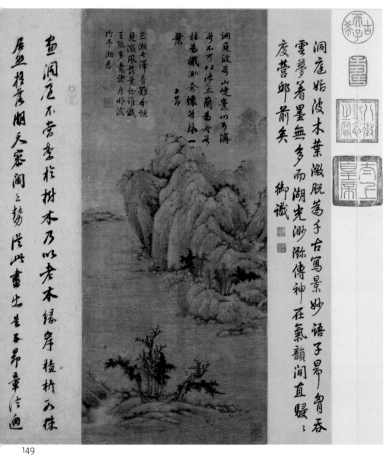

149

149 Eastern Peak of Dongting

Zhao Mengfu (1254–1322)
Yuan
Hanging scroll, ink and colour on silk
Height 60.8 cm, Width 26.6 cm

Zhao Mengfu was an artist and writer from
Wuxing (present-day Huzhou, Zhejiang Province).
He took the style name Zi'ang, the literary names
Songxue and Shuijinggong Daoren, and was
called Wenmin posthumously. As a scion of the
Song imperial family he was a court official under
both the Song and Yuan. His calligraphy and
painting both show great accomplishment. He
believed that 'it is important for paintings to have
an ancient feel', and this influenced subsequent
generations of painters.

This painting is skilfully composed with the
Eastern Peak of the Dongting Mountains in the
centre, which reaches out on a peninsula into the
still waters of Lake Tai. The low trees set off the
grandness of this lake, one of the five largest in
China. The brushstrokes of mountains, rocks,
trees and leaves are after the style of the Tang
painter Dong Yuan (active 935–62). The ripples of
water, the art of colouring and composition have
the feel of paintings from the Tang period.

There is a poem on the right hand of the
painting, with the signature 'Zi'ang' and a red seal,
'Zhao Shi Zi'ang' (Zi'ang of the Zhao family). Li Lan

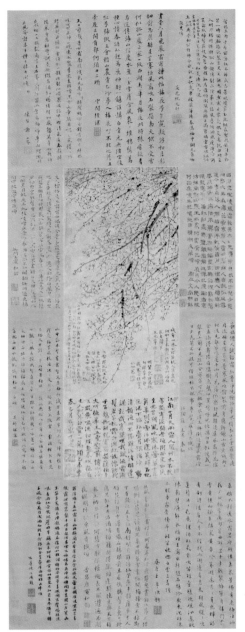

150

151

152

150 Black Plum Blossom
Wang Mian (?–1359)
Yuan
Hanging scroll, ink wash on paper
Height 67.7 cm, Width 25.9 cm

151 Singing while Sailing in Autumn
Sheng Mao (14th century)
Yuan
Hanging scroll, ink and colour on silk
Height 167.5 cm, Width 102.4 cm
Donated by Wei Tingyun.

152 Drinking Together under the Pines
Tang Di (1286–1364)
Yuan
Hanging scroll, ink and colour on silk
Height 141.1 cm, Width 97.1 cm

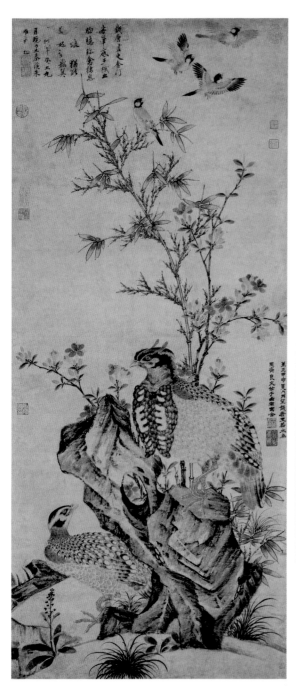

153

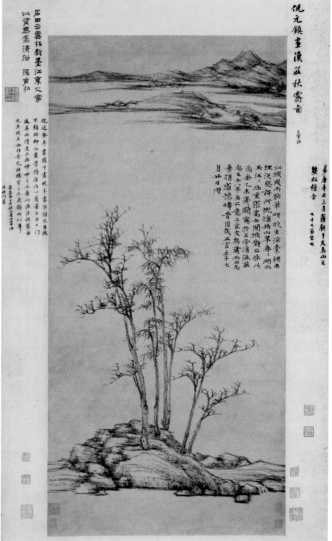

154

---

153 Bamboo, Rock and Birds
Wang Yuan (14th century)
Yuan
Hanging scroll, ink wash on paper
Height 137.5 cm, Width 59.4 cm

**154 Fishing Village on a
Clear Autumn Day**
Ni Zan (1301–74)
Yuan
Hanging scroll, ink wash on paper
Height 96.1 cm, Width 46.9 cm

155 Retreat in the Qingbian Mountains
Wang Meng (1308–85)
Yuan
Hanging scroll, ink on paper
Height 140.6 cm, Width 42.2 cm

Wang Meng's style name was Shuming and he took the literary names Xiangguang Jushi and Huanghe Shanqiao. He was a native of Wuxing (present-day Huzhou, Zhejiang Province) and was accomplished in both calligraphy and paintings, especially landscapes of exuberant mountain scenes. His influence on later generations was considerable and, with Ni Zan, he is known as one of the 'Four Masters of the Yuan period'.

This painting depicts the Bian Mountains in the northwest of Wuxing County near Lake Tai. The composition uses a method known in Chinese landscape painting as the 'three distances'. It shows towering mountain peaks, rugged and steep but covered in exuberant and verdant vegetation. There is a human figure walking in the wood and others sitting in the cottage in the middle distance. The painting reflects the leisurely and carefree lifestyle of the literati in retreat from political life. The brushwork is exquisite and different painting techniques are used to depict the mountains, rocks, trees and vegetation. The ink density and the composition give the perfect combination of paint and space.

This was chosen as the best work of this artist by the art critic Dong Qichang (1555–1636), who also painted the Bian Mountains. It was painted in the 26th year of Zhizheng reign (1366) when the artist was 59. Li Lan

155

156

**156 Visiting my Friend Dai
on a Snowy Night**
Zhang Wo (14th century)
Yuan
Hanging scroll, ink on paper
Height 91.1 cm, Width 39.3 cm

157

157 Lotus and Mandarin Ducks
Zhang Zhong (14th century)
Yuan
Hanging scroll, ink on paper
Height 147 cm, Width 56.8 cm

158

159

---

158 Flower, bamboo and birds
Bian Wenjin (active 1426–35)
Ming
Hanging scroll, ink and colour on silk
Height 155 cm, Width 99 cm

**159 Verdant Mountains
in the Spring**
Dai Jin (1388–1462)
Ming
Hanging scroll, ink on paper
Height 141 cm, Width 53.4 cm

160

160

160

160

160 Flower, Birds, Grass and Insects (in four sections)
Sun Long (15th century)
Ming
Albums, ink and colour on silk
Height 22.9 cm, Width 21.5 cm

161 Camellia with White-feathered Birds
Lin Liang (c. 1416–c. 1480)
Ming
Hanging scroll, ink and colour on silk.
Height 152.3 cm, Width 77.2 cm

161

162

163

163 Beauties (two sections: Chuiwan and Jiuju)

Du Jin (15th–16th century)
Ming
Handscroll, colour on silk
Height 30.5 cm, Width 168.9 cm

Du Jin had the style name Junan and the literary name Qingxia Ting Zhang (Elder of the Qingxia Pavilion). He was a native of Dantu (present-day Zhenjiang, Jiangsu Province) and was a poet, writer and painter, but excelled in line drawing.

This work references Zhou Wenju's (active 961-75) *Court Life*, depicting various aspects of the daily life and entertainment of the imperial concubines. *Chuiwan* was a ball game popular from the Song and Yuan periods where the players tried to hit a ball into a hole, reminiscent of western golf. It was very popular among Ming aristocrats. The painting shows a ball which has stopped right next to the hole. The player lowers her head and bends her knee, with her club hand extending out. *Jiuju* is an ancient football game. There are many images of women playing *jiuju* on bronze mirrors and porcelain pillows of the Tang, Song and Yuan periods but this painting depicts the three person version of the game which was popular during the Ming.

The painting bears the red seal 'Qingxia Ting', but no signature.
TIAN SUMIN

162 Farewell at Jingkou

Shen Zhou (1427–1509)
Ming
Handscroll, ink on paper
Height 30 cm. Width 125.5 cm
Donated by Shen Tongyue.

164

164 Yellow Crane Tower
An Zhengwen (Ming period)
Ming
Hanging scroll, ink and colour on silk
Height 162.5 cm, Width 105.5 cm

165 Summer Day in a Mountain Village
Zhou Chen (15th–16th century)
Ming
Hanging scroll, ink and colour on paper
Height 113.5 cm, Width 59.2 cm

166 Repose under a Pine
Wu Wei (1459–1508)
Ming
Hanging scroll, ink and colour on silk
Height 166.8 cm, Width 97.2 cm

165

166

167

167 Zhenshang Studio

Wen Zhengming (1470–1559)
Ming
Handscroll, ink and colour on paper
Height 36 cm, Width 107.8 cm

Wen Zhengming, a Ming period calligrapher and painter,
was originally called Wen Bi but was known by his style
name, Zhengming. His other style name was Zhengzhong
and he took the literary name Hengshan Jushi. He was a
native of Wuxian (present-day Suzhou, Jiangsu Province). He
specialised in landscapes and is one of the so-called 'Four
Masters of the Ming'.

Zhenshang Studio was the study of Hua Xia, a famous
collector from Wuxi. On this painting, the cottage is situated
on flat ground next to a winding lake surrounded by hilly
slopes, rugged garden rocks, pines and bamboo groves. This
is a typical Southern Chinese garden. Inside the cottage, the
host and his guests look at paintings and discuss literature,
typical pursuits of the literati. The brushstrokes are
meticulous yet vigorous and the colour light and elegant.
Following the painting is an inscription on Zhenshang Studio
written by Wen Zhengming, in both regular and official
scripts.

This painting is in perfect condition. It was painted in the
jiyou year of the Jiajing reign period (1549) when the artist
was 80. Tian Sumin

詳細看大都誰不逐炎凉
秋來紈扇合收藏何事佳人重感傷請托深情
晉昌唐寅

168 Lady with Fan in the Autumn Breeze

Tang Yin (1470–1523)
Ming
Hanging scroll, ink on paper
Height 77.1 cm, Width 39.3 cm

Tang Yin's style name was Bohu and his literary name was
Liuru Jushi. He was a native of Wuxian (present-day Suzhou,
Jiangsu Province). Skilled in both calligraphy and painting, he
specialised in landscapes and figures with fine lines. He is
one of the so-called 'Four Masters of the Ming'.

Tang Yin went to Beijing to attend the imperial civil service
examinations when he was thirty, but he was dismissed
from his office because of cheating after which he was
shunned by friends and family. Tang Yin used his poetry and
paintings to express his disappointment with the snobbish
world.

In this painting, a pensive lady holding a fan stands on a
slope, her dress dancing in the autumn wind. She is lifelike
and beautiful, her face and hair drawn with delicate and
refined brushstrokes. The painting succeeds in being both
vigorous as well as gentle, and is an excellent example of
Tang Yin's later work. TIAN SUMIN

168

169

170

170

170

170

169　Two Birds

Lu Ji (15th–16th century)

Ming

Hanging scroll, ink and colour on silk

Height 128.4 cm, Width 84.9 cm

170　Flowers (four sections)

Chen Daofu (1483–1544)

Ming

Album, ink on paper

Height 28 cm, Width 37.9 cm

Donated by Liu Jingji

171

171   Bamboo and Beauty
Qiu Ying (?–c.1552)
Ming
Hanging scroll, ink and colour on silk
Height 166.8 cm, Width 97.2 cm
Donated by Yang Diemian.

**172   Paying Respect to the
Ancients on Mount Li**
Wen Boren (1502–75)
Ming
Hanging scroll, ink and colour on paper
Height 152 cm, Width 47 cm

172

173   Mount Wudang after Snow
Xie Shichen (1487–1567)
Ming
Hanging scroll, ink and colour on silk
Height 88.3 cm, Width 62.2 cm

武當積雪宮喬春

174

174 Flowers and Fruit (one section)
Xu Wei (1521–93)
Ming
Handscroll, ink and colour on paper
Height 33.5 cm, Width 522.8 cm

175 Landscape after a Poem in Xixia Temple
Dong Qichang (1555–1636)
Ming
Hanging scroll, water and ink on paper
Height 133.1 cm, Width 52.5 cm

176 Deep Autumn on Mount Hua
Lan Ying (1585–?)
Ming
Hanging scroll, ink and colour on silk
Height 310.9 cm, Width 102.2 cm
Donated by Wei Tingyun.

175

176

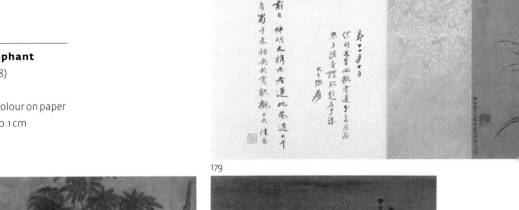

177 Washing an Elephant

Ding Yunpeng (1547–1628)

Ming

Hanging scroll, ink and colour on paper

Height 115.1 cm, Width 50.1 cm

177

178

179

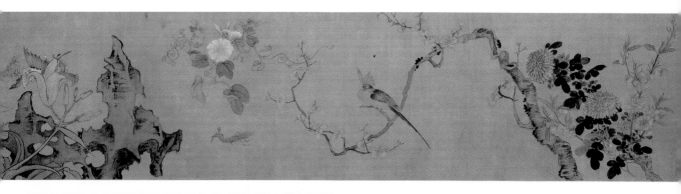

180

180　Valued Friends

Xiang Shengmo (1597–1658) and Zhang Qi (late Ming)
Ming
Hanging scroll, ink and colour on paper
Height 38.1 cm, Width 25.5 cm

Xiang Shengmo was from Xiushui (present-day Jiaxing, Zhejiang Province) and took the style name Kongzhang and the literary name Yi'an. He was renowned for his paintings of landscapes, flowers, trees, bamboos, rocks and figures, but his speciality was painting pines ('song' in Chinese) and for this reason he was called 'Xiang Song'. Zhang Qi, whose style name was Yuqi, was also from Xiushui and specialised in portraits.

Zhang Qi painted the portraits in this painting and Xiang Shengmo added the landscape and inscriptions. It shows an episode in Xiang's life when he was 40 years old and went on an art appreciation tour with five literati friends. The figure in red, shown holding one end of a handscroll, is the famous painter Dong Qichang (see 4.40). Sitting next to him is his good friend, the artist Chen Jiru. Xiang stands behind Chen. The other three figures are the monk Zhixuan, painter and connoisseur Li Rihua and his pupil Lu Dezhi. They talk about art and Chan Buddhism while sitting in this sylvan scene.

It was painted in the 9th year of the Shunzhi reign period (1652) when Xiang Shengmo was 59. TIAN SUMIN

178　Fusheng Teaching Buddhist Scriptures

Cui Zizhong (d.1644)
Ming
Hanging scroll, ink and colour on silk
Height 184.4 cm, Width 61.7 cm

179　Flower, Birds, and Insects

Chen Hongshou (1598–1652)
Ming
Handscroll, ink and colour on silk
Height 32.6 cm, Width 161.5 cm

181

182

181   Stream and Mountains in the style of Juran
Wang Jian (1598–1677)
Qing
Hanging scroll, ink and colour on paper
Height 88.6 cm, Width 50.8 cm

182   Listening to Orioles among Green Trees
Kuncan (1612–93)
Qing
Hanging scroll, ink and colour on paper
Height 118.9 cm, Width 32.9 cm

183

184

183 Washing an Ink Stone in a Stream
Hongren (1610 – 1663)
Qing
Handscroll, ink and colour on paper
Height 19.7 cm, Width 69.7 cm

184 Five Scenes of Nanjing
Fan Qi (1616 – after 1694)
Qing
Handscroll, ink and colour on silk
Height 30.1 cm, Width 60 cm

185

185 Trees in Autumnal Colours
Gong Xian (1618–89)
Qing
Hanging scroll, water and ink on paper
Height 99.5 cm, Width 64.8 cm

186 Twelve Scenes of Mount Hua (detail)
Dai Benxiao (1621–94)
Qing
Album, ink and colour on paper
Height 21.2 cm, Width 16.7 cm

186

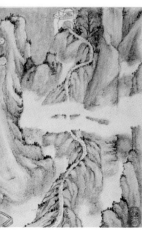

187

187 Mount Jingting after Rain
Mei Qing (1623–97)
Qing
Hanging scroll, ink on paper
Height 171.7 cm, Width 63.6 cm

188 Two Eagles
Zhu Da (1626–1705)
Qing
Hanging scroll, ink on paper
Height 172.7 cm, Width 90.8 cm

189 Forest Place of the Immortals
Wang Hui (1632–1717)
Qing
Hanging scroll, ink and colour on paper
Height 84 cm, Width 39.9 cm

190 Spring Lake
Wu Li (1632–1718)
Qing
Hanging scroll, ink and colour on paper
Height 123.5 cm, Width 62.5 cm

188

189

190

191

192 Pines in Fine Rain

Shitao (1641–after 1707)

Qing

Hanging scroll, ink and colour on paper

Height 100.8 cm, Width 41.3 cm

Donated by Shen Tongyue, Gu Fo, Gu Duxuan, Gu Liu, Gu Duzhang and Gu Duqiu.

Shitao was a calligrapher, painter, art theorist and a Buddhist monk. Named Zhu Ruoji, he came from Quanzhou in Guangxi Province and was a scion of the Ming imperial family. His Buddhist name was Yuanji, but he is generally known by his style name Shidao. He also had several literary names including Da Di Zi and Monk Kugua. He specialised in landscapes, flowers – especially orchids – fruits and bamboos. He was also good at figure painting and had a significant influence on later generations. He is known as one of 'The four eminent monks of the early Qing'.

This work was painted in his midlife. It depicts Huangshan (Mount Huang) in fine rain, with old pine trees and waterfalls. It is rare to see Shitao's fine-brushed work like this. The rocks and mountains are outlined with dark ink, the brushstrokes are fresh, elegant and vigorous. The distant mountains are painted with square outlines while the slopes and rocks in the foreground are painted with rounded edges and flowing brushstrokes. The colours of the painting are light brown and blue, clean and elegant.

It was painted in the 26th year of the Kangxi reign period (1687) when the artist was 47. Li Lan

191 Flowers (detail)

Yun Shouping (1633–90)

Qing

Albums, ink and colour on silk

Height 29.9 cm, Width 22.2 cm

192

193

**193　Cloud and Mountains
in the Style of Gao Kegong
(1248–1310)**

Wang Yuanqi (1642–1715)
Qing
Hanging scroll, ink and colour on paper
Height 113.6 cm , Width 54.4 cm

194

195

---

194 Eagle and pine painted by finger
Gao Qipei (1660–1734)
Hanging scroll, silk on paper
Height 161.1 cm, Width 74.7 cm

---

195 Streams in late Spring
Yuan Jiang (17th century–early 18th century)
Hanging scroll, ink and colour on silk
Height 104 cm, Width 49.5 cm

196 Peacocks
Shen Quan (1602– after 1762)
Hanging scroll, ink and colour on paper
Height 239.5 cm, Width 123 cm

196

197 Golden Valley Garden
Hua Yan (1682–1756)
Qing
Hanging scroll, ink and colour on paper
Height 178.9 cm, Width 94.1 cm
Donated by Shen Tongyue, Gu Fo, Gu Duxuan, Gu Liu, Gu Duzhang and Gu Duqiu.

198 Lotus
Li Shan (1686–after 1757)
Qing
Hanging scroll, ink on paper
Height 125.9 cm, Width 60.9 cm

199 Plum Blossom
Jin Nong (1687–1763)
Qing
Hanging scroll, ink on paper
Height 119 cm, Width 31.5 cm

197

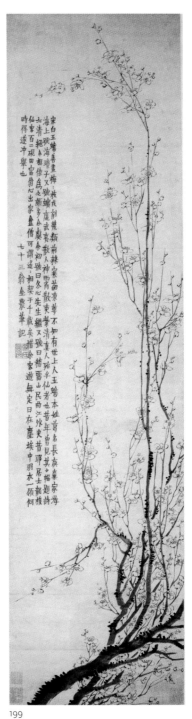

198

199

200 Auspicious Bouquet

Lang Shining (Giuseppe Castiglione) (1688 – 1766)
Qing
Hanging scroll, ink and colour on silk
Height 109.3 cm, Width 58.7 cm

Giuseppe Castiglione was born in Milan, Italy and joined the Jesuit order at 19. He had produced European oil paintings before he left for China in 1714 where he served in the court of the Kangxi emperor and was known as Lang Shining. He specialised in painting portraits and horses, combining Western and Chinese methods. His brushwork was very refined but he used intense colours.

This painting shows a bouquet of flowers, symbolising good luck, in a beautiful vase. The petals and leaves are painted with in mixture of shades giving them a three-dimensional realistic feel, reminiscent of western still lives.

It was painted at the 3rd year of the Yongzheng reign period (1725) when the artist was 38. TIAN SUMIN

200

201 Bamboo and Rock

Zheng Xie (1693–1765)
Qing
Hanging scroll, water and ink on paper
Length 217.4 cm, Width 120.6 cm

202 Fish Playing in Spring Waves

Xu Gu (1821–1896)
Qing
Hanging scroll, ink and colour on paper
Length 127.4 cm, Width 39.9 cm

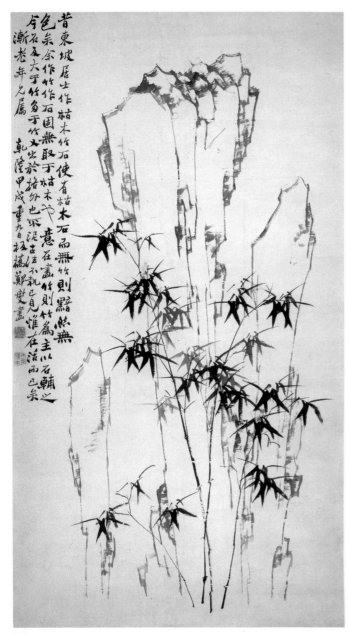

201

202

203

204

205

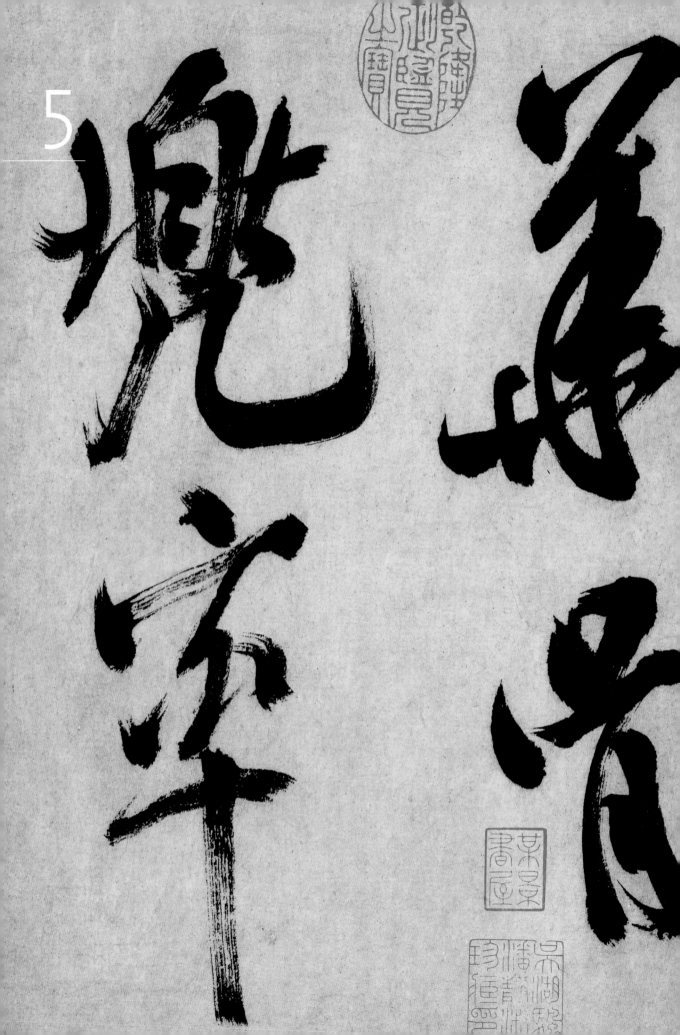

5

CALLIGRAPHY

The calligraphy collection of the Shanghai Museum is very rich and contains many masterpieces from different periods. The most renowned pieces include the works by the fourth-century Wang Xizhi and his son Wang Xianzhi, namely *The Shangyu Letter* and *The Yatouwan Letter*, both in cursive script; *The Kusun Letter* in cursive script by Huaisu of the Tang; *The Poem on The Pavilion of Many Views* in running script by Mi Fu and *The Response to the Literary Discussion with Xie Minshi* in running script by Su Shi of the Northern Song; *The Autumnal Mood Poem* in running script by Zhao Mengfu of the Yuan, and *Ode of the Red Cliff* in cursive script by Zhu Yunming of the Ming. Many pieces are the only extant copies in history, for example *The Thousand Character Classic* in cursive script by Gao Xian of the Tang. Gao Xian was an eminent monk from the mid Tang period who specialised in cursive scripts. His work is extremely rare to find, this masterpiece is the only extant copy and has great historical value.

The Ming and Qing calligraphy collection can compete with the painting collection in both its quantity and quality. Two collections compliment each other and form a comprehensive history of the painting and calligraphy of the Ming and Qing period.

Over the last few years the Shanghai Museum has also held many large-scale special exhibitions on ancient Chinese calligraphy, including 'Rare Editions of *Chun Hua Ge Tie*', 'Treasures of Chinese and Japanese Calligraphy' and others. These exhibitions aroused great interest from Chinese and overseas scholars and researchers, and an international audience. LI LAN

207

---

207 *Kongzi Shilun* **(Confucius's Discussion of Poetry)**
Warring States
Bamboo slips
Height 55 cm, Width 0.6 cm

---

208 *Zhouyi* **(Book of Changes)**
Warring States
58 bamboo slips
Height 44 cm, Width 0.6 cm

This copy of the classical text on divination, *Zhouyi*, was written on bamboo strips in the Warring States period before the Qin emperor's proscription of Confucian texts. It is the earliest copy of this text discovered to date and is one of the most important books from this period. The Shanghai Museum purchased it on the Hong Kong antique market in 1994 and its exact provenance is therefore uncertain. It consists of 58 slips which contain 1806 characters on 34 of

206

---

206 **Oracle bone**
Shang period
Ox scapula
Length 35.5 cm, Width 13.7 cm

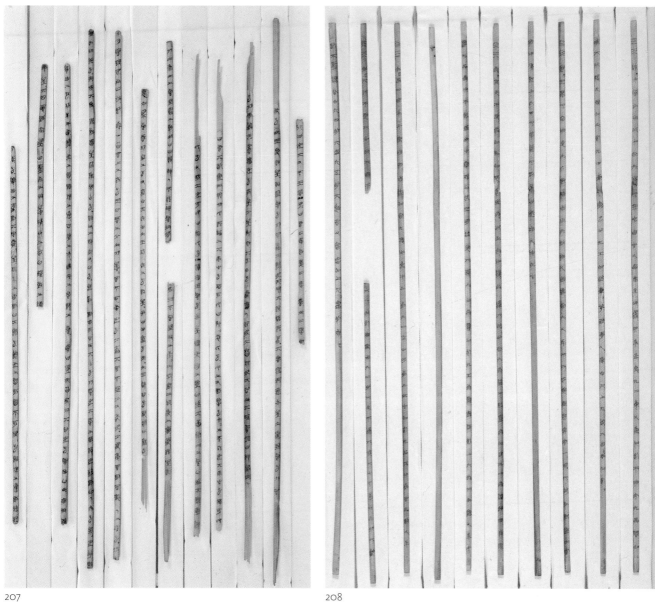

207

208

the hexagrams or divinatory diagrams in the *Zhouyi*. There are three so-called 'combined characters' where two characters are combined into one, and ten places where only the first of two repeated characters is given. The slips also have illustrations of 25 hexagrams. The intact slips are 44 cm long and were originally attached by three strings. Although some slips have been lost, we can still reconstruct the main contents of the pre-Qin *Zhouyi*. Especially interesting are a set of divinatory symbols which are not found in the post-Qin versions. The form and contents of these symbols each have their own meaning which include the interaction between *yin* and *yang*.

This book is in three sections: the hexagrams, text and symbols. The text is completely different both from the post-Qin *Zhouyi* silk book excavated from Mawangdui and from received versions.

There are six forms of symbols presented in red and black. The section on each hexagram is in five parts: a picture of the diagram, its name, its initial symbol, an explanation of the diagram and its lines, and the final symbol. There is a space after each end symbol indicating that the diagrams are mutually independent. The book is written in the script of the Chu state and there is no commentary.

PU MAOZUO

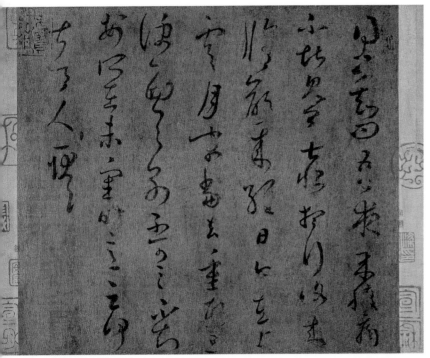

209

209 *The Shangyu Letter*, running and cursive

Wang Xizhi (307–65), Tang period copy
Handscroll, ink on paper
Height 23.5 cm, Width 26 cm

Wang Xizhi was from Langye (in present-day
Shandong Province), but lived mainly in Kuaiji
(present-day Shaoxing, Zhejiang Province). His
style name was Yishao. He reached the official
rank of Chief Administrator of Kuaiji and General
of the Right Army, and is also known as 'Right
Army Wang'. He created a fluent and elegant style
of his own in both running and cursive scripts, and
in the Tang period he was honoured as 'the sage of
calligraphy'. He made a great contribution to the
development of Chinese calligraphy by revering
tradition while creating a new style.

The Shangyu Letter was originally written by
Wang Xizhi in running and cursive script. This is a
Tang period copy. It is named after the phrase
'Nowadays in Shangyu...' which appears in the
letter. The brushstrokes are forceful and elegant
and the traces of the old cursive style can still be
seen in many characters. The style is typical of
Wang Xizhi's running and cursive script in his later
years.

The calligraphy bears the seals of many
collectors, including red imperial seals *Nei he tong
yin* (Imprint of the Court) from the Southern Tang
and *'Yushu'* (Emperor's Hand) from the Song.
LI LAN

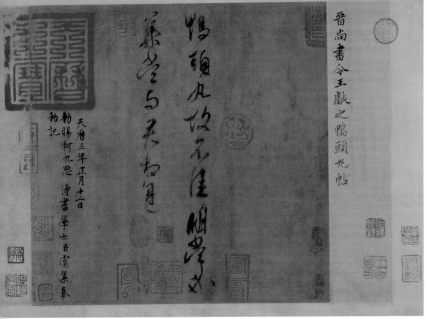

210

210 *The Yatouwan Letter*, running and cursive

Wang Xianzhi (344–88)
Eastern Jin
Handscroll, ink on silk
Height 26.1 cm, Width 26.9 cm

211

211 *The Kusun Letter*, **cursive script**
Huaisu (737–99)
Tang
Handscroll, ink on silk
Height 25.1 cm, Width 12 cm

Huaisu, originally surnamed Qian and from Changsha, was a Buddhist monk with the ordination name 'Zang Zhen' (Treasury of the Truth). He was famous for his wild cursive script and had a great influence on later generations.

Kusun, bitter bamboo, is a plant growing in the southwest part of China. This letter consists of fourteen characters in two lines reading: 'The combination of bitter bamboo and tea is exceedingly good. Please send more. Regards, Huaisu.' It is exquisitely written in both cursive and running scripts, with flexible well spaced brushstrokes showing coherent movement. The style has a vigorous charm, described by the Chinese phrase, 'birds flying from the forest, snakes sliding into grass.'

This work was in the collections of the Song emperor in the Xuanhe period (1119–26) and the Southern Song Shaoxing period (1131–63) and is a rare Huaisu manuscript.
Li Lan

212

212 *Ningzhou Letter*, zhen **script**
Sima Guang (1019–86)
Northern Song
Handscroll, ink on paper
Height 32.7 cm, Width 57.6 cm

213 *A Precis of Suramgama*
Samadhi Sūtra, running **script**
Wang Anshi (1021–86)
Northern Song
Handscroll, ink on paper
Height 29.9 cm, Width 119 cm
Donated by Fang Shuyan.

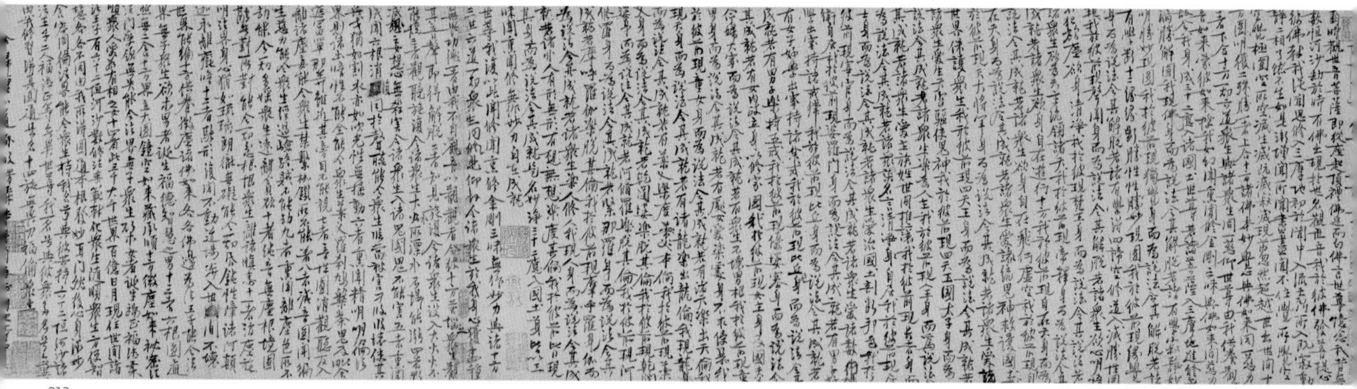

213

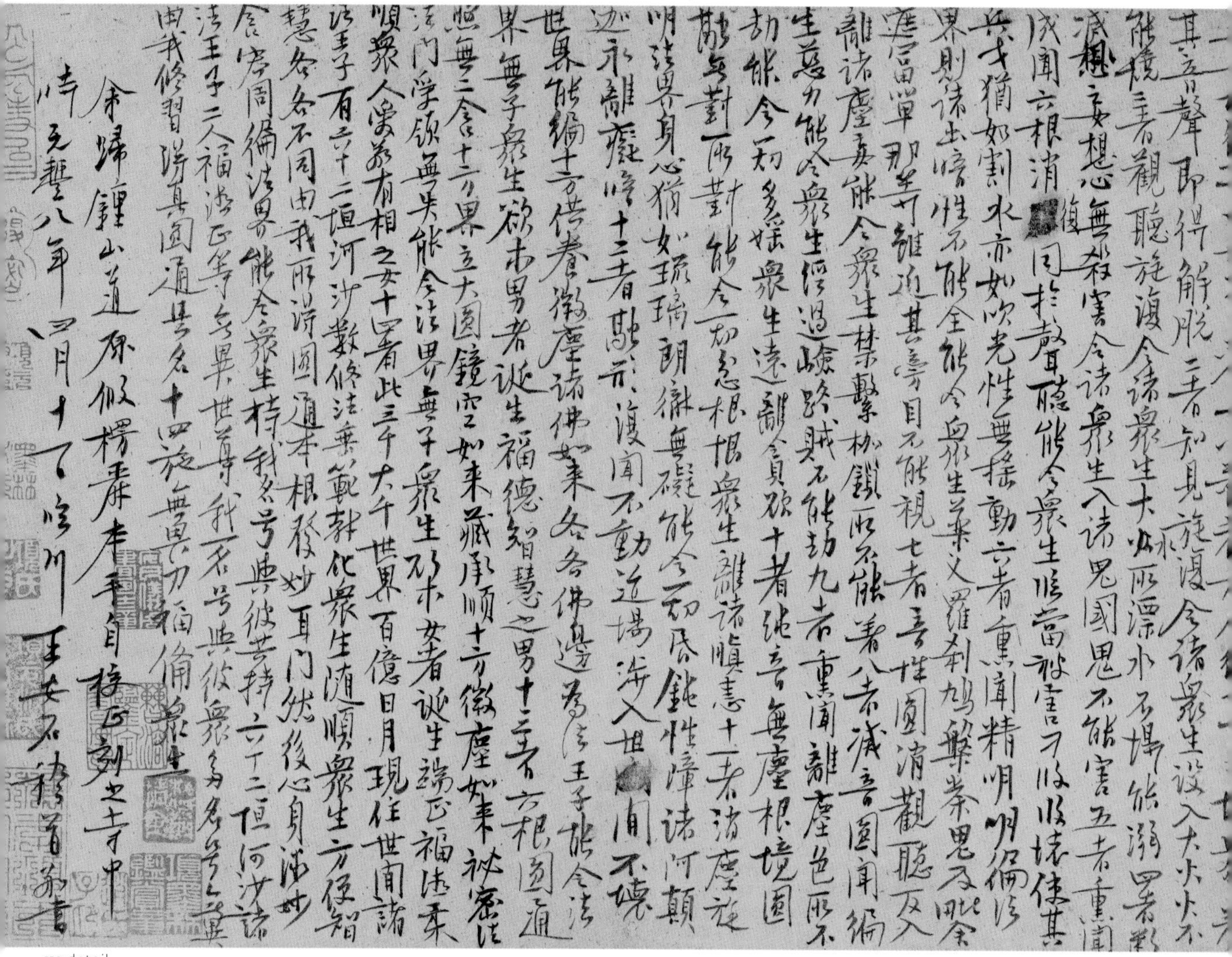

213 detail

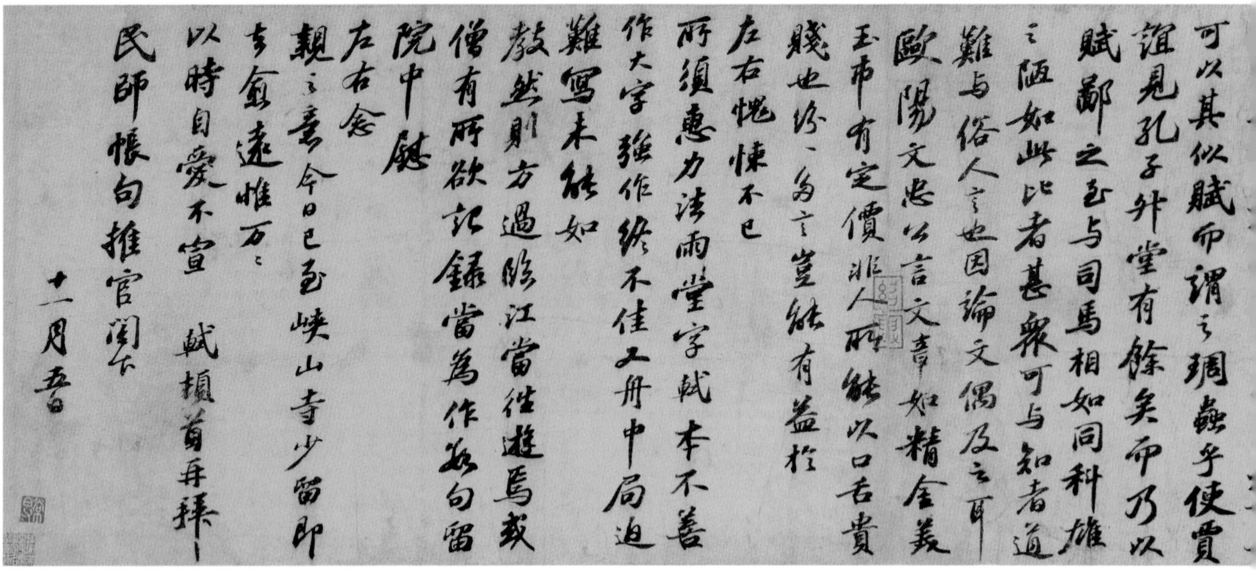

214

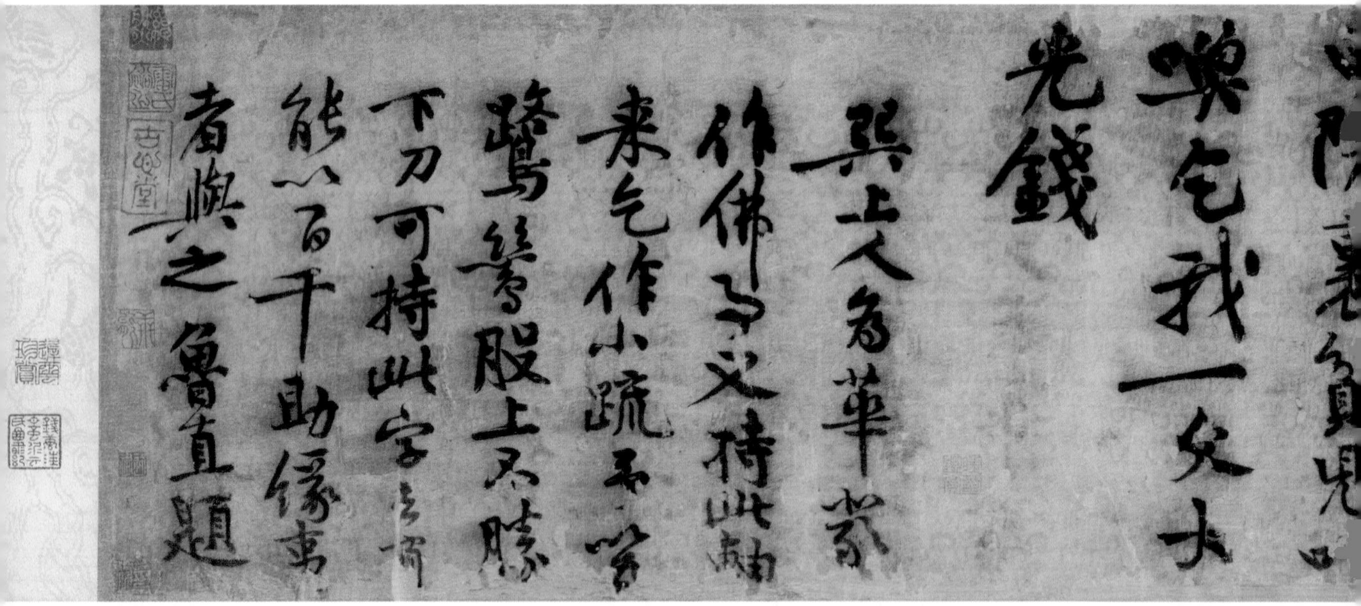

215

215 *Avataṃsaka Sūtra,*
running script
Huang Tingjian (1045–1105)
Nothern Song
Handscroll, ink on silk
Height 25.1 cm, Width 115 cm

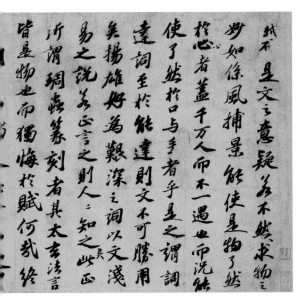

214 *Response to the Literary Discussion with Xie Minshi, running script*

Su Shi (1036–1101)
Northern Song
Handscroll, ink on paper
Height 27 cm, Width 96.5 cm

Su Shi was from Meishan in Meizhou (present-day Sichuan Province) and was a famous writer, painter and calligrapher. His style name was Zizhan and he took the literary name Dongpo Jushi. His calligraphic speciality included both running and regular scripts. He was one of the so-called 'Four Masters of the Song' together with Huang Tingjian (1045–1105), Mi Fu (1051–1107) and Cai Xiang (1012–67).

The handscroll is missing the first 158 characters, the extant section consisting of 33 lines, with 360 characters. The text differs slightly from the version in the handed-down *Collection of Dongpo's Works*. The piece ends with the line: 'Here Shi again pays his respects to Mr Xie Minshi. 5th day of the 11th month." The calligraphy has a classic and vigorous style, sincere yet spontaneous, with plump brushstrokes. Li Lan

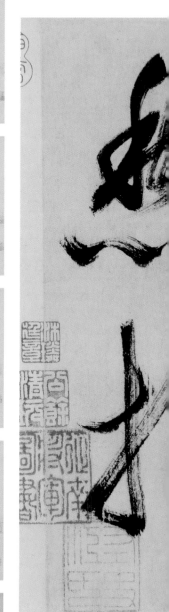

216

216 *Poem on The Pavilion of Many Views (Duojing Lou)*, **running script**
Mi Fu (1051–1107)
Northern Song
Album, ink on paper
Height 31.2 cm, Width 53.1 cm

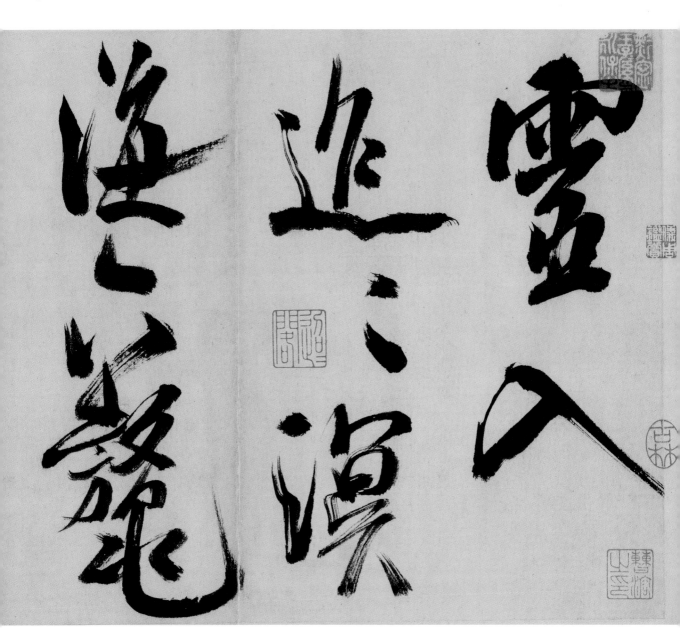

216 detail

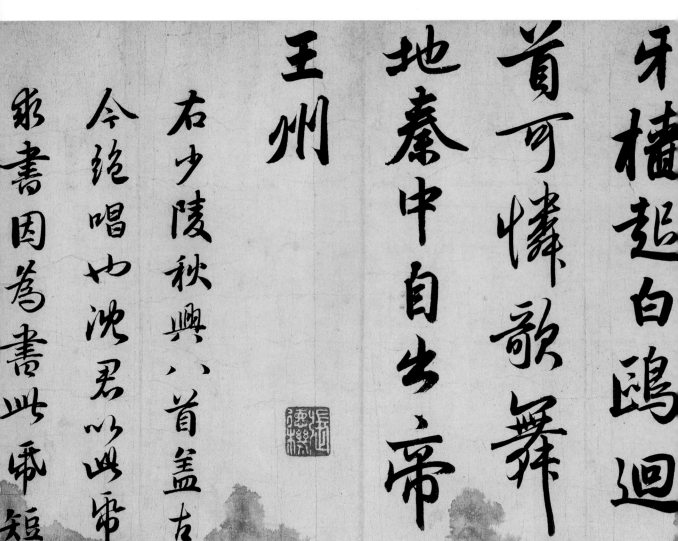

217 detail

217

**217　*Autumnal Mood Poem,*
running script**

Zhao Mengfu (1254–1322)
Yuan
Handscroll, ink on paper
Height 23.5 cm, Width 261.5 cm

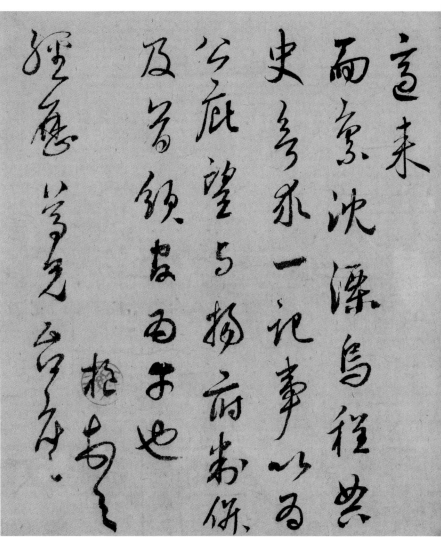

218

**218 *The Shilai Letter*,
running script**

Xianyu Shu (1257–1302)
Yuan
Album, ink on paper
Height 26.2 cm, Width 24.4 cm

219 *Seven Character Regulated Poem*, cursive script

Yang Weizhen (1296–1370)

Yuan

Hanging scroll, ink on paper

Height 107.7 cm, Width 34.9 cm

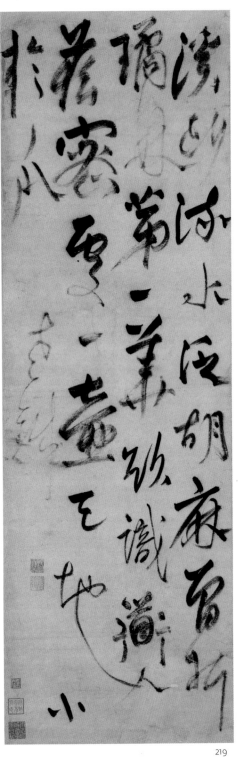

219

220 detail

220

220

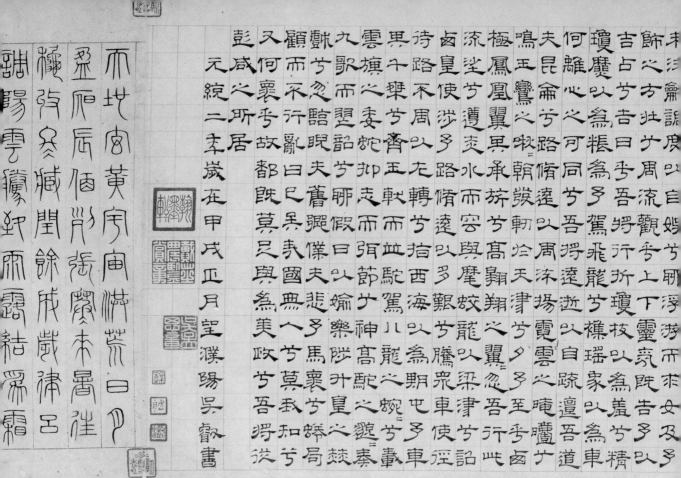

220 Book of Seal Script and Official Script (details, one from each section)
Wu Rui
Yuan
Handscroll, ink on paper
Height 28.2 cm, Width 425.1 cm

221 *Taking Leave of Wu Zhongyu,* cursive style

Zhang Bi

Ming

Hanging scroll, ink on paper,
Height 107.9 cm, Width 33.9 cm

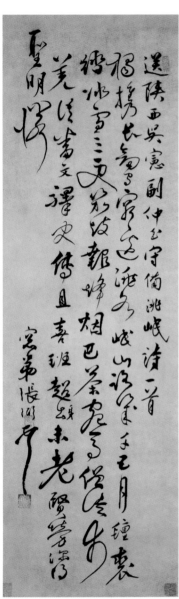

221

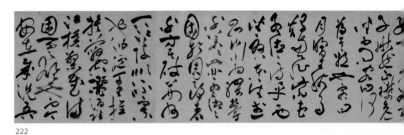

222

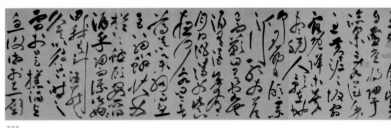

222

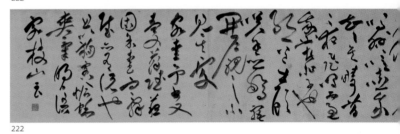

222

222 detail

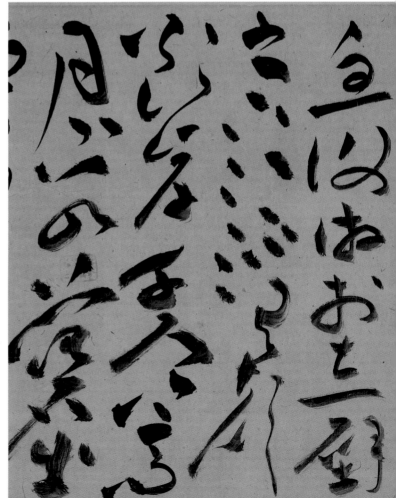

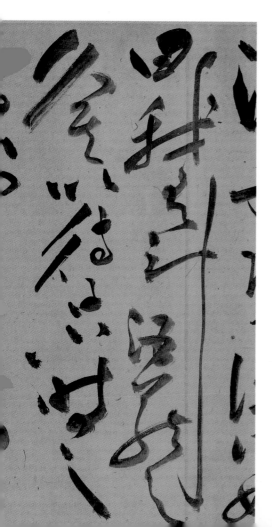

222 *Ode of Red Cliff*, cursive script

Zhu Yunming (1460–1526)
Ming
Handscroll, ink on paper
Height 31.3 cm, Width 1001.7 cm

Zhu Yunming, style name Xizhe and literary name, Zhishan, was from Changzhou (present day Suzhou, Jiangsu).

This work contains two poems entitled *Ode of Red Cliff*, totalling 156 characters. The whole piece is written in a freehand cursive script, following the style of Zhang Xu (c.658–748) and Huaisu (see 5.5). It is full of emotion. Both the tip and the side of the brush are used to write characters which differ greatly in size but flow together without a break. Some characters are represented simply by dots.

The scroll contains colophons and postscripts by artists such as Wen Zhengming. It is a masterpiece of Zhu Yunming's calligraphy, and an excellent example of the wild cursive scripts from the mid Ming period.
Li Lan

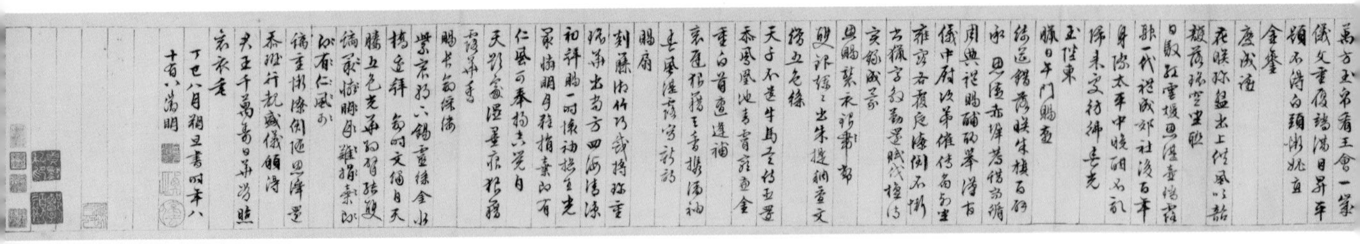

雨中放朝

飛湍号澗泛霓旌歷廣

非墀散暖聲照色浮煙迷

左揆珞雲將雨上西清扮

香壽殉子鎮重水甍銀橋

萬玉鳴珂濕石窮袍袖濕

玉術産津馬踹距

早朝

月揚蕎訢瀾甬西建章

雪劍玉遲怪路業雙引

齊老幸濁行班石陛深嚴

寄坳細綵扇于分雉尾

通籍頭金闕日高歸浣詞

頸心湯袖□香拆宗泳

雪後長安門候朝

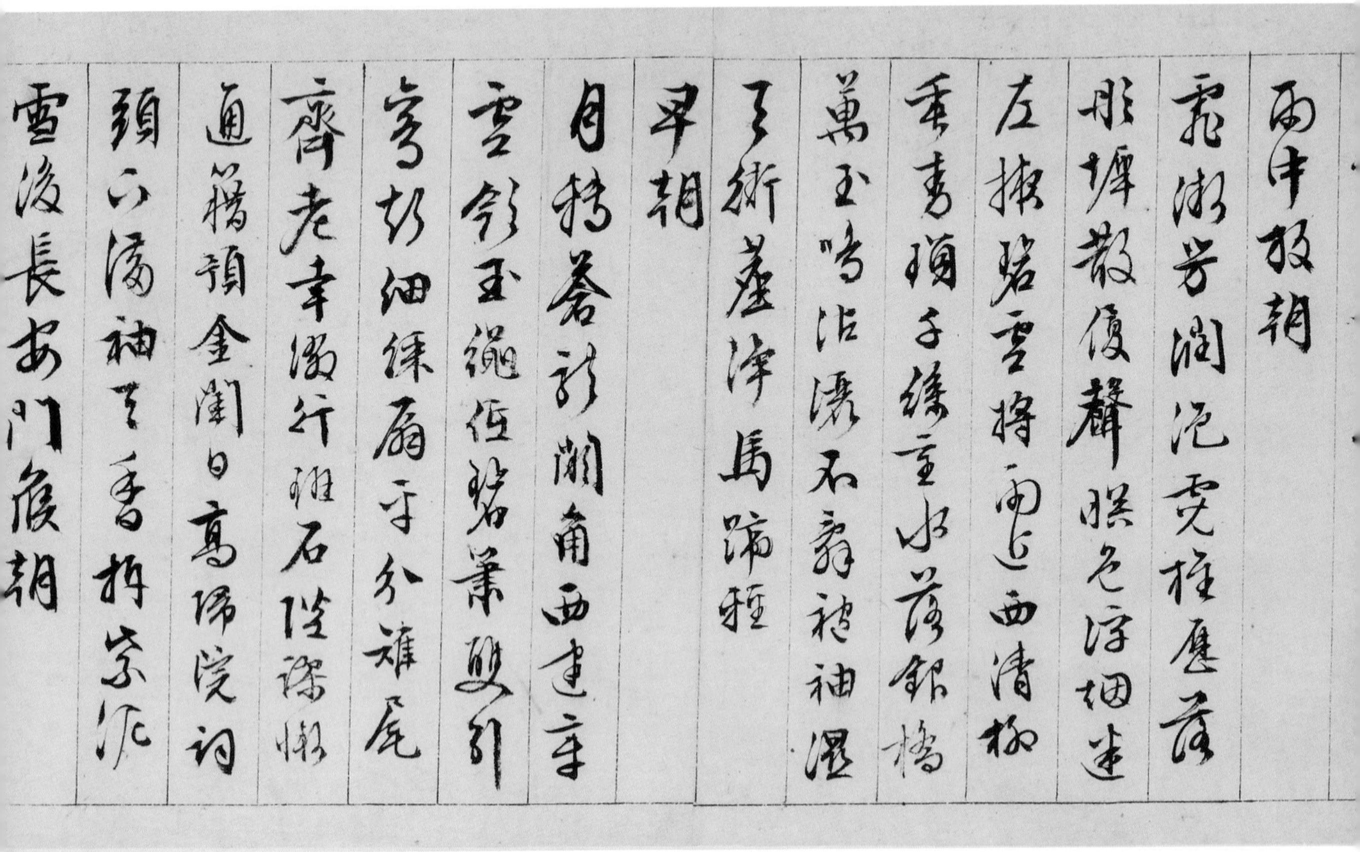

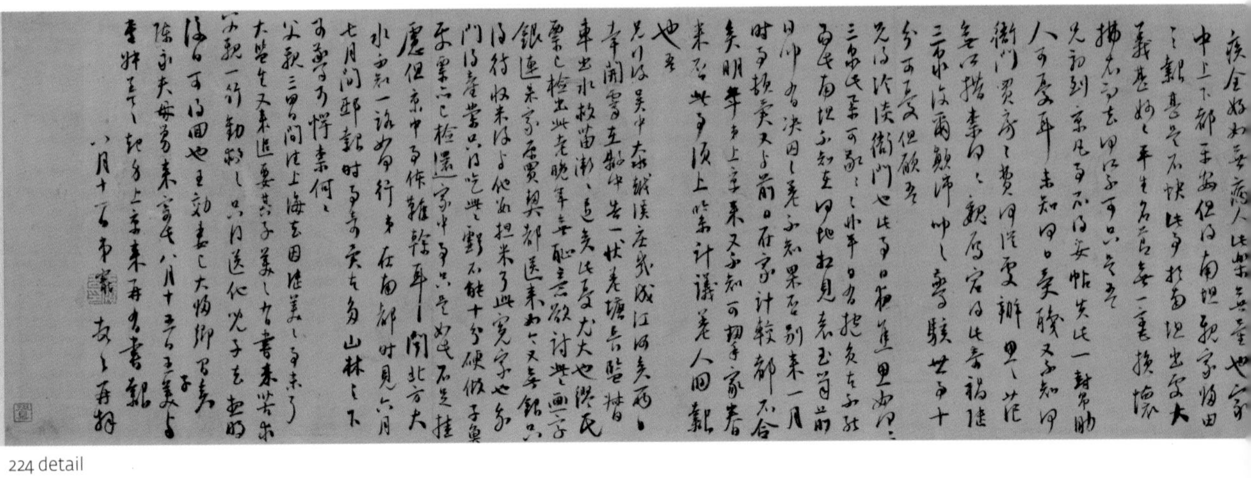

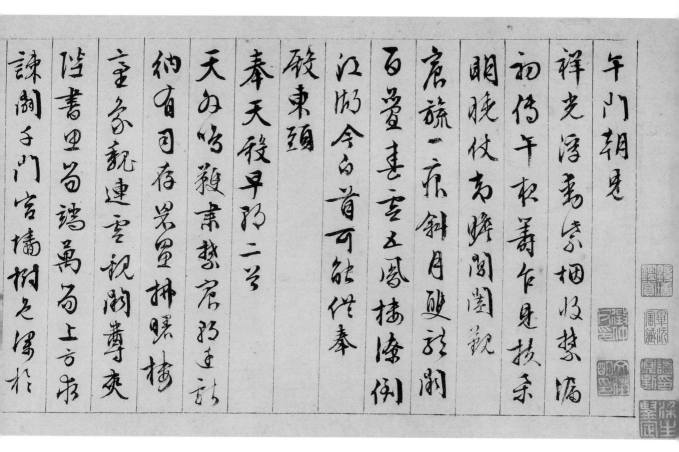

223   Poem, running script
Wen Zhengming (1470–1559)
Ming
Handscroll, ink on paper
Height 20 cm, Width 249 cm

224   Yuezhi Lun, regular script
Wang Chong (1494–1533)
Ming
Handscroll, ink on paper
Height 19.9 cm, Width 59.8 cm
Donated by Sun Ding.

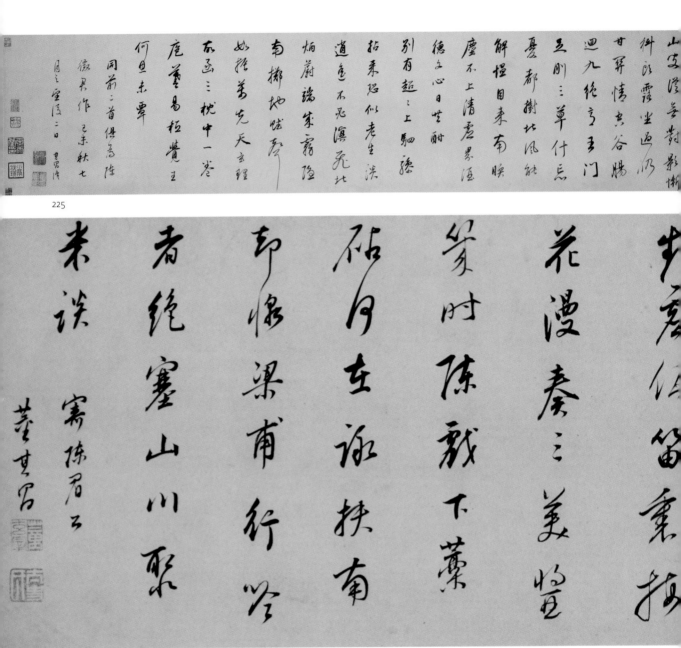

225

225 detail

225 *Poem Dedicated to Chen Meigong*, running script
Dong Qichang (1555–1636)
Ming
Handscroll, ink on paper
Height 25.9 cm, Width 112.7 cm

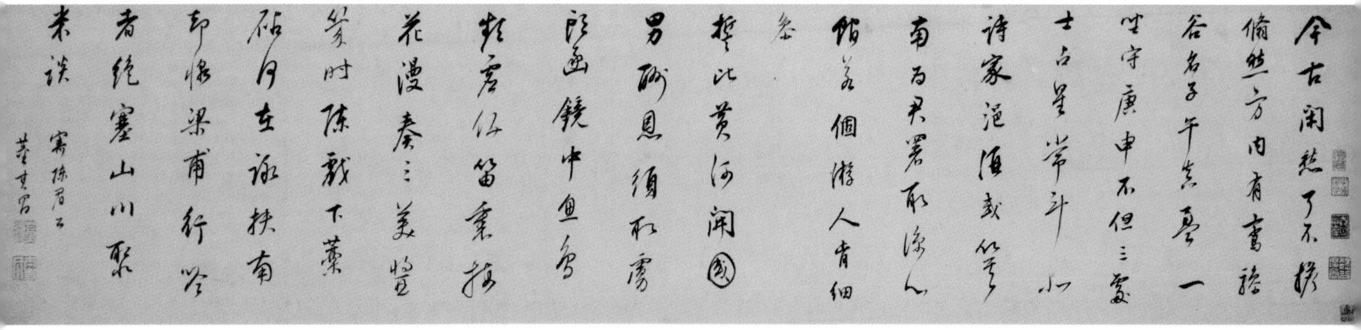

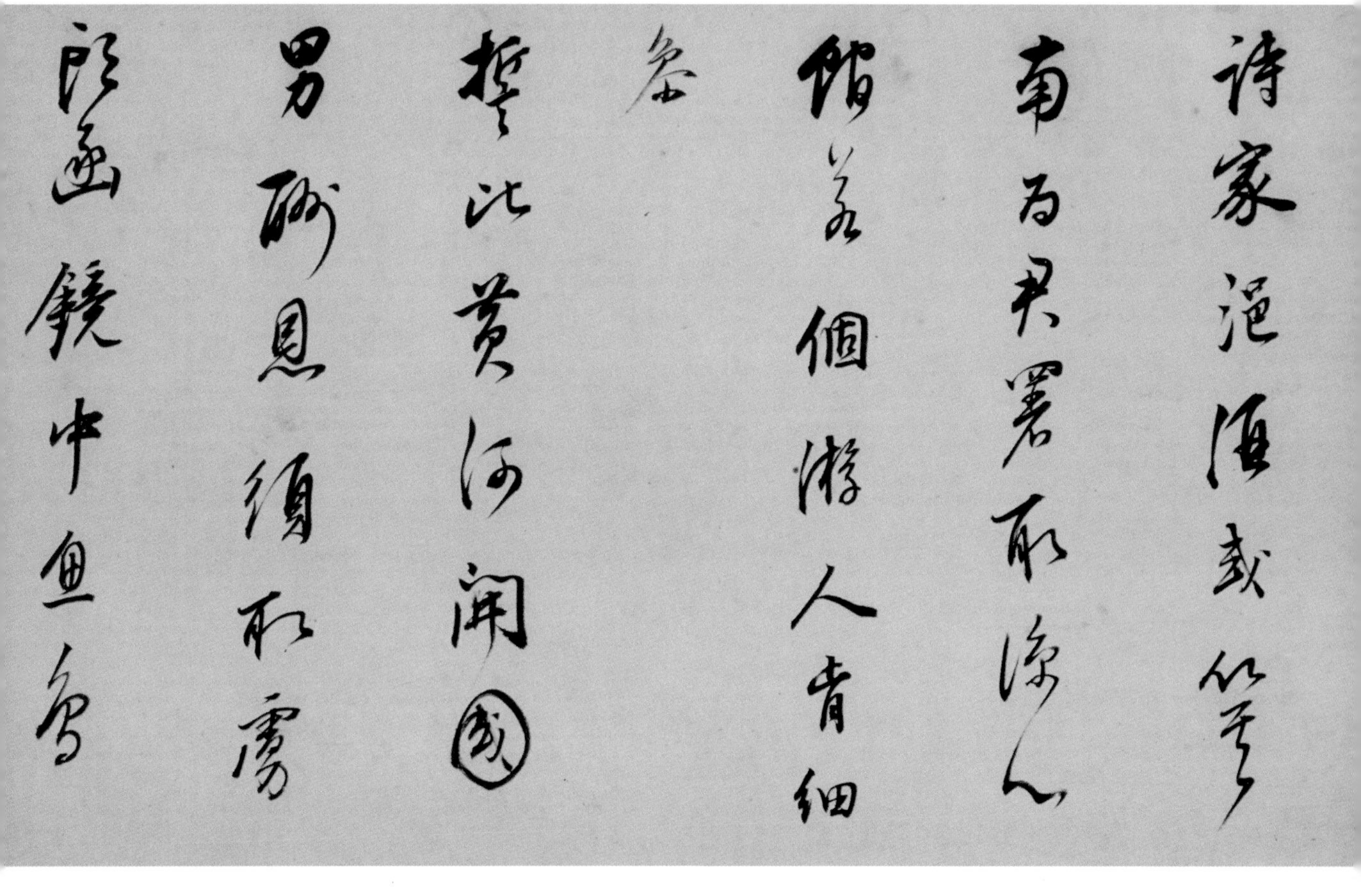

今古閑愁了不禁
偷然方内有青鞋
各各子平宗夢一
坐宇庚申不但三家
士占星常斗小
詩家泡酒或筆
南為某署耶深人
偕兰個游人青細
冬
挈此黄河闹國
男城恩須不雪
幽鏡中魚兮
鑒時陳載下葉
花漫奏三美豐
非君任留棄指
硯月左誼扶南
即臨梁甫行吟
者統塞山川聚
米誤
寄陳君石
董其昌

226 *Five Character Regulated Poem*, running script

Fu Shan (1607–84)

Qing

Hanging scroll, ink on silk

Height 201.6 cm, Width 52.3 cm

Donated by Yang Diemian.

227 *Four Character Poem*, running script

Wang Duo (1592–1652)

Qing

Hanging scroll, ink on silk

Height 300 cm, Width 51.8 cm

228 *Poem After the Melody of Huanxisha*, official script

Zheng Fu (1622–93)

Qing

Hanging scroll, ink on paper

Height 173.6 cm, Width 89.6 cm

229 *Five Character Four Line Poem*, running script

Kangxi emperor, Xuan Ye (1661–1722)

Qing

Hanging scroll, ink on gold paper

Height 135.8 cm, Width 58.2 cm

Donated by Yang Diemian.

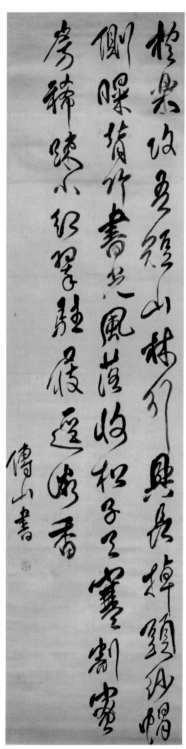

226

227 >

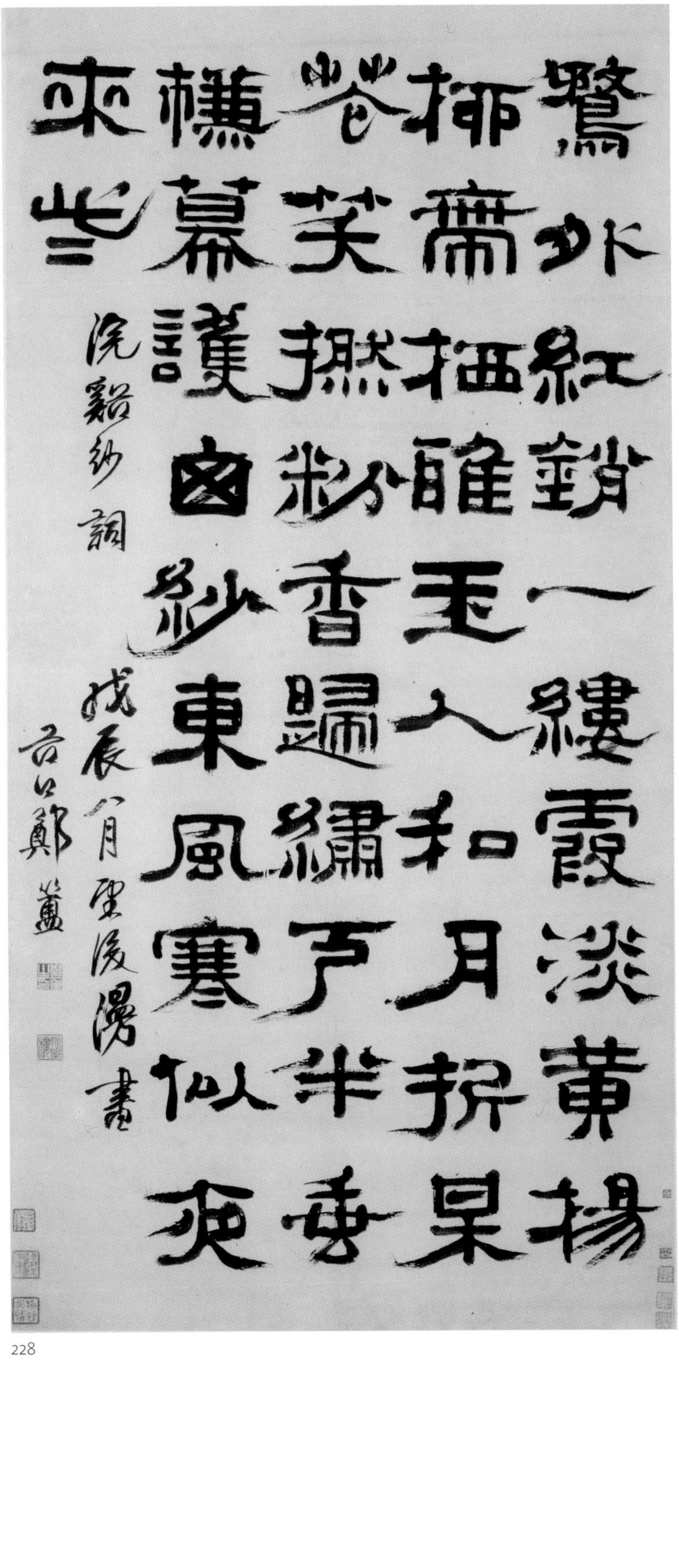

來坐 樵幕護謢 卷芙茉撚粉 挪簾撫雎玉 驚水下紅綃一縷霞淡黄楊
浣谿紗調 紗 香歸綉戶 人和月拆垂柳
戊辰月望後漫書 東風寒似 半
古郡鄭蕙書 爽 垂 杲楊

228

山月皎如燭雲風時動
竹衣半掩勸撫窗中
人獨宿
臨董

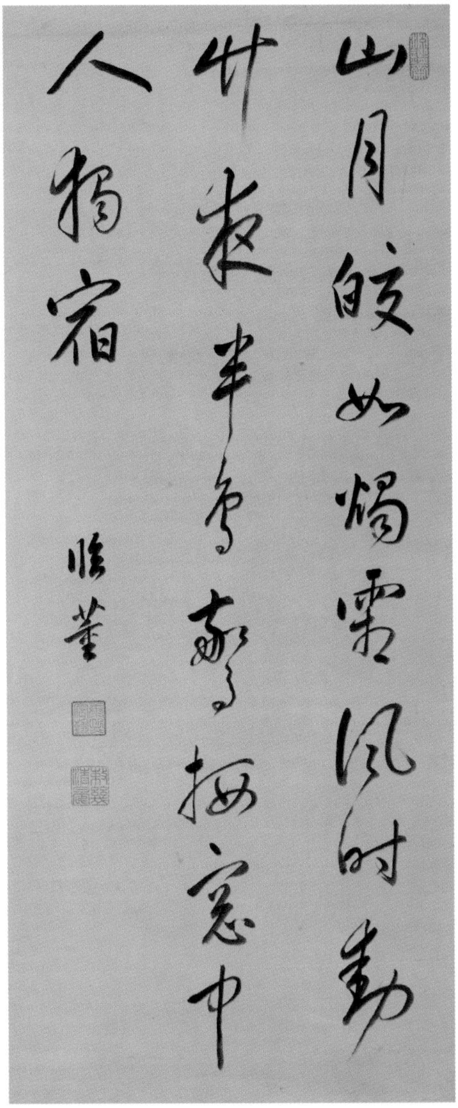

229

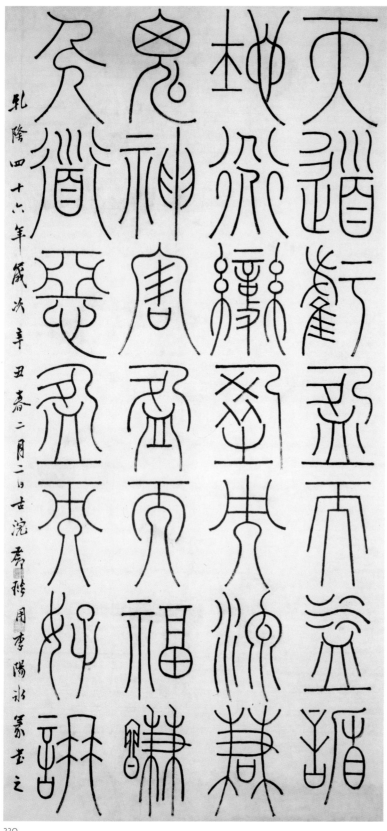

230

230 *On the Hexagram Qian*, seal script

Deng Shiru (1743–1805)
Qing
Hanging scroll, ink on paper
Height 168.8 cm, Width 84.3 cm
Donated by Hong Fu.

Deng Shiru, from Huaining, Anhui Province, was originally named Deng Yan, and took the style name Wanbo and the literary name Wanbai Shanren. He was accomplished in all four scripts of calligraphy, especially *zhuan* or seal script. He was also an expert seal carver and his style was honoured as the 'Deng School'.

This work is on *qian*, one of the sixty-four hexagrams from the *Zhouyi*. The brushstrokes are clean and precise. Deng Shiru disregarded the early Qing fashion for writing *zhuan* script using very fine lines, and instead returned to the Qin and Han style of using much thicker strokes. He innovatively added stylistic features from Han rubbings, so creating a new school and aesthetic in Qing calligraphy.

At the bottom of the scroll there is the colophon: 'On the second day of the second month in the spring of the 64th year of the Qianlong reign period (1871), Deng Yan from Anhui writes this in the *zhuan* script in the style of Li Yangbing.' He was 39 years old. LI LAN

231 *Seven Character Couplets*, running script

Yi Bingshou (1754–1815)
Qing
Hanging scroll, ink on paper
Height 131.6 cm, Width 29.3 cm

232 *Five Character Regulated Poem*, running script

Wu Changshuo (1844–1927)
Qing
Hanging scroll, ink on paper
Height 128 cm, Width 33.7 cm

盃酒今應一哂用
嘉慶丁卯曹日 汀州弟伊秉綬

舊書不厭百回讀
山民仁兄待詔正之

磬折間惝到詩談老自妄魯維巖對
語我七硯加磬夢幔來呼園維魚可釣
礚石磬樓高百尺姹素倚闌干
小詩就
夢波先生指正戊午六月吳昌碩

6

Chinese seals combine the arts of calligraphy and carving and are praised in Chinese for showing 'thousands of variations within a square inch'. Rudimentary seals appeared during the Shang and Zhou periods. They were then put to wider use as tallies during the Spring and Autumn and the Warring States periods. Seal making gradually became recognized as an art form with particular attention paid to the script forms, the design of the knob and the aesthetic feel of the material. Literati seal carving during the Ming and Qing periods retained the formality of ancient seal carving tradition while adding individual characteristics and thus many different schools and genres were formed.

The Shanghai Museum's seal collection, comprising around 13,000 items, is special as it is comprehensive and representative of Chinese seal history. It includes ancient imperial seals, signature seals and seals made by eminent artists from the Ming and Qing periods. SUN WEIZU

233

233

234 Bronze seal with a tortoise shaped knob
'Sui xiu shen shui wei zhu zhong shi wu' 岁宿申水为助中士五

Wang Mang interregnum (9-25)

Length 2.4 cm

Width 2.4 cm, Height 2.25 cm

Donated by Hua Du'an and Mao Mingfen.

This seal is historically very interesting. 'Zhong Shi' was a military post instituted under the short reign of Wang Mang, and was subordinate to a General or a Commander-in-Chief. Other characters in the inscription on this seal do not appear in the names of official ranks under any other Chinese dynasty. *The History of the Han Dynasty (Hanshu)*, 'Biography of Wang Mang', records that in the first year of the Gengshi reign period (23 AD) 'the armies of Wang Mang and Liu Xiu met in a great battle at Kunyang (present-day Yexian, Henan). Wang Mang's army was close to defeat but Wang Mang used astrological and geomantic techniques to try to win back the advantage. He sent soldiers to destroy the tomb of the Han emperor Yuan on the Wei River, and that of Han emperor Cheng at Yan. He ordered the perimeter wall painted black and changed the titles of his military officers. The general (*jiangjun*) was named 'Assisted by the star god Jupiter of the "shen" branch and water element' (*Sui xiu shen shui wei zhu*). He ordered the people 'to take large axes, cut down dead trees, clear the water flow and extinguish all fire.' It is further recorded in the chapter 'On Astronomy' that 'the country under the influence of Jupiter can not be conquered, and will conquer other countries.' Wang Mang sought to exploit these astrological predictions. Each new dynasty had a dominant element and that of the Han dynasty was fire, while his rule was under the element of earth. Because water would overcome fire, he added the water element to the General's title. The remainder of his changes were all based on these theories, common beliefs at the time.

According to the inscription, this seal was issued after the Kunyang Battle in the late Western Han period. The fibres on this seal indicate that it was wrapped in silk before being buried. Another seal acquired at the same time by the Museum reads 'Jiangjun Zhongshi wu xu' (Deputy General). The two seals have similar patterns of verdigris and similar forms, suggesting that they were produced at the same time. They provide the only evidence of Wang Mang's tactics based on these beliefs.
SUN WEIZU

233 Bronze seal
'Qiu hou qi ma' 逎侯骑马 (Cavalry Officer, the Duke of Qiu)

Western Han period

Length 7.8 cm

Width 7.6 cm

Height 5.25 cm

234

234

235　Jade seal 'Wei ba' 魏霸

Eastern Han

Length 2.9 cm

Width 2.9 cm

Height 2.0 cm

236　Stone seal carved by Xu Dongyan

'Ji feng hong fu ke yu qiu ran'

妓逢红拂客遇虬髯

Ming

Length 2.55 cm

Width 3.05 cm

Height 6.5 cm

Donated by Hua Du'an and Mao Mingfen.

235

235

236

236

237

237

237   Gilded silver seal with *qilin* shaped knob 'Duo luo ding jun wang yi' 多罗定郡王印 (Seal of the Prince of Duo Luo Ding)

Inscription in both Chinese and Manchu, two lines and six characters each

Qianlong reign period, Qing

Length 10.8 cm

Width 11 cm

Height 11.8 cm

The Qing Manchu imperial house carried on Chinese tradition whereby there were twelve titles bestowed upon the emperor's sons and grandsons, including 'Imperial Prince', 'Commandery Prince', and, the lowest, 'General by Grace'. According to *The Draft History of the Qing (Qing shi gao)*, in the 37th year of the Qianlong reign period (1772), the emperor bestowed the title 'Prince of Duo Luo Ding' on his great-grandson Miande, son of Imperial Prince Yonghuang. The title was passed on to Yonghuang's younger son Mianen, his great-grandson Sun Zaiquan and great-great-grandson Sun Fuxi through to the 33th year of the Guangxu reign period (1907).

There were strict regulations governing the making of a prince's seal. 'The seal of the Prince of Duo Luo Ding must be made from gilded silver with a *qilin* knob, 3.4 inch square and one inch thick.' Its inscriptions must be in both Chinese and Manchu.

Qing imperial seals were hereditary and are extremely rare. This one was made during the Qianlong reign period. The *qilin* is delicately wrought with a serious demeanour. Regulations on the imperial treasures of the Qing house stipulated that only the emperor, empress, imperial princes and princesses and their descendants could use seals with coiled dragons, intertwined dragons, squatting dragons, tortoise and *qilin* knobs. SUN WEIZU

238 Mao Xiang Pijiang's (1611–93) personal seal carved by Dai Benxiao (1621–91), with inscriptions on six sides

Qing
2.75 × 2.25 cm
Height 4.55 cm
Donated by Mei Yin and others.

Mao Xiang, a native of Rugao, Jiangsu Province, was a writer, painter and calligrapher with the style name Pijiang and the literary name Chaomin ('nest dweller'). Together with Fang Yizhi, Chen Zhenhui and Hou Fangyu, he was one of the 'Four Noble Sons of the Ming'. He did not pass the imperial examinations but was a member of a politico-literary society which opposed an influential court eunuch. Although he was later offered an official post he refused and spent time at his Shuihui Retreat, entertaining friends with wine and theatre, while enjoying and creating poetry, paintings and calligraphy. He was celebrated for his romantic image and literary grace.

The seal carver, Dai Benxiao, was also a celebrated figure. Together with artists Mei Qing, Mei Geng and Shitao, they were the elite of the Huangshan (Yellow Mountain) School of landscape painting. Mao Xiang also commissioned Xu Rong, a seal carver of the Rugao School, to make six-side seals for his concubine Cai Han and his son Mao Jiahui, using the same stone. All three seals remained in the Mao family for many generations.

This seal is inscribed on all six sides with two sides containing two seals each. The inscriptions read 'Mao Xiang Pijiang si yin' (personal seal of Mao Xiang); 'Chaomin' (Mao Xiang's style name); 'Mao Xiang'; 'Pijiang shi' (Mao Xiang's literary name); 'Zhenshang' (Appreciator of the truth); 'Xiao San wu jian cang' (Xiao San wu jian collection); and 'ren rong wang yuan' (to endure disgrace and forgive). One side is inscribed with a phoenix-shaped bell.

Ming and Qing literati were particularly interested in the shape and the playfulness of a seal. Many seals emulated ancient styles but others show great creativity in their form. This seal gathers eight seals in one, each a different shape – square, round, rectangular, oval and gourd-shaped. Each could be used in different circumstances making this an innovative and practical design.

Sun Weizu

238

239

239

239

239   Stone seal carved by Huang Yi
(1744–1802) '*Xiaosong suode*'
(in the collection of Xiaosong)
Qing
2.4 × 2.4 cm
Height 5.9 cm
Donated by Hua Du'an and Mei Mingfen.

240

240 Stone seal carved with a cloud and dragon design by Wu Changshuo (1844–1927) 'Tianyou tang' (The Hall of Celestial Travel)

5 × 5 cm
Height 16.0 cm
Donated by Kang Baozhuang and Kang Bao'e.

Wu Changshi was from Anji, Zhejiang Province, and took several literary names including Foulu. He was a poet, painter, seal carver and calligrapher but in his later years was already earning a good living from his art and usually passed on commissions for seal carvings to his second son Wu Han. Wu Changshi would write the inscription, leave the carving to his son, then add the final touches and sign his name. This seal was made like this. It has the signature on the side: 'Carved for the Gentleman of Nanhai, first month of the *guihai* year, in the 80th year of old man Fou'.

The seal was carved for the famous Qing reformer, Kang Youwei (1858–1927) who came from Nanhai, Guangdong Province, and whose studio name in his later years was 'Tianyou Tang' (The Hall of Celestial Travel). After his reforms failed Kang Youwei was forced into exile abroad for sixteen years and travelled widely, hence his studio name. He returned to China in 1914 and settled on Yuyuan Road in Shanghai where he knew many artists and writers. Sᴜɴ Wᴇɪᴢᴜ)

7

ANCIENT CHINESE JADE

Jade plays a key role in Chinese civilisation and although jade carving is also an art of the native American and Maori cultures, neither can rival Chinese jade for its history, variety, quality and carving skills. China was not only the first culture in the world to make and use jade, but the stone was also linked from the earliest times with religious, ritual and political influence. Not only did it have a decorative function, it was also used as a symbol of wealth and power, for talismans by rulers making offerings to heaven and earth, instruments of communication with the ancestors and a charm for the dead to fend off evil spirits.

Jade adornments have been found at excavated sites belonging to the Xinglongwa Culture of the Liao River region in Inner Mongolia dating from c.6200–5400 BC. The Hongshan Culture (c.3500–2200 BC) and the Liangzhu Cultures (c.3400–2250 BC) were also adept at jade making, reaching high standards in selecting material, decorating, carving and polishing. Jade carved animals from the Hongshan Culture and sacrificial jade objects from the Liangzhu were forms that continued in Chinese jade in later periods. Ritual jade developed hugely during the Erlitou, Shang and Zhou periods while jade ornaments became more popular during the Spring and Autumn, Warring States and Western Han periods. Different forms were developed to match the rank, status and identities of emperors, princes and nobles. Later on, from the Tang and Song period, jade ceased to be so associated with magical powers, being used for everyday objects by ordinary people and those produced in the Liao and the Jin periods are particularly distinctive. During the Yuan, the Ming and the Qing periods, there was more variety in jade forms and subjects, starting with straightforward styles showing simplicity and power, but gradually developing into the much more elaborate and large jade sculptures of the Qing. HUA CIXIANG

241 Penannular ring
Majiabang Culture (5000–3700 BC)
Diameter 3.1 cm
Excavated from the lower stratum of
the Songze site, Qingpu County,
Shanghai, 1976.

241

242

**242 *Cong* with anthropomorphic masks and flying
birds pattern**
Liangzhu Culture
Diameter 6.6 cm
Height 5 cm
Excavated at Fuquan Shan, Qingpu County, Shanghai, 1982.

A *cong* is a tube of square cross section pierced with a circular hole that
was made as a ritual object, although its exact function and meaning is
still unclear. This *cong* is made from a lake green translucent jade. An
anthropomorphic mask, with two circles as eyes and a horizontal bar
as its nose, is carved on each corner. Two protruding long bars at the
top serve as the crown and fine geometric patterns are carved on the
bar. On both sides of each mask are two bird designs. A *cong* with this
type of design is typical of Liangzhu Culture. Hua Cixiang

243 Axe
Liangzhu Culture
17.1 × 10.9 cm
Excavated at Fuquan Shan, Qingpu
County, Shanghai, 1982.

244 Anthropomorphic head
Longshan Culture (c.3000–1700 BC)
Width 3.6 cm
Height 6.2 cm

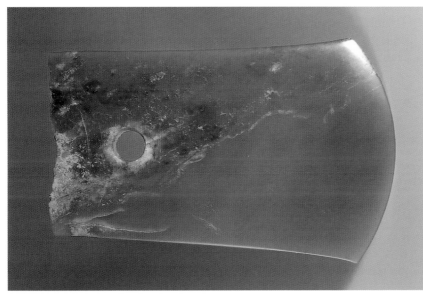

243

244

245 Axe with face design
Late Shang (13th – 11th century BC)
8.3 × 5.4 cm

246 Tiger
Late Shang (13th – 11th century BC)
Length 9.5 cm
Height 2.4 cm

245

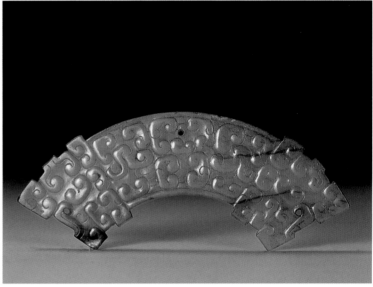

247

247 Pendant with double dragon design
Spring and Autumn Period
Length 10.6 cm
Width 3 cm

246

248

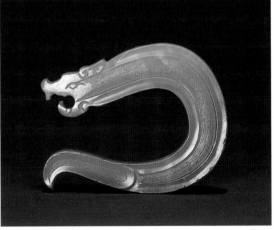

249

248   Ornament with phoenix and dragon design

Western Zhou
Length 12.6 cm
Width 4.7 cm

This piece of decorative green jade is discoloured from water damage during burial. The design shows a phoenix on top, with a curved beak, and crest and long tail. Below it is a coiled dragon with large staring eyes. The design is the same on both sides. The carving is vigorous and fluent, using a combination of single intaglio lines and slanting lines. This carving technique was a Western Zhou innovation.
HUA CIXIANG

249   Dragon

Warring States
Height 3.2 cm
Width 4.2 cm

The C-shaped dragon is carved from a green jade with yellowish-brown blotches. The outline of the dragon is incised and the body decorated with fine and intersecting zigzag patterns. There are two drilled holes on the neck and the tail of the dragon, enabling this to be linked with other pieces and it therefore probably belongs to a set of jade adornments. HUA CIXIANG

250

250 Sheath with dragon and phoenix design
Warring States
Length 7.2 cm
Width 2.4 cm, Height 3.1 cm

251 *Bi* (ritual disc) with bird design
Western Han
Diameter 14.6 cm

252 Ornament with design of the four magical animals (dragon, tiger, phoenix and deer)
Eastern Han
Length 5.5 cm
Width 2.1 cm, Height 3.2 cm

251

252

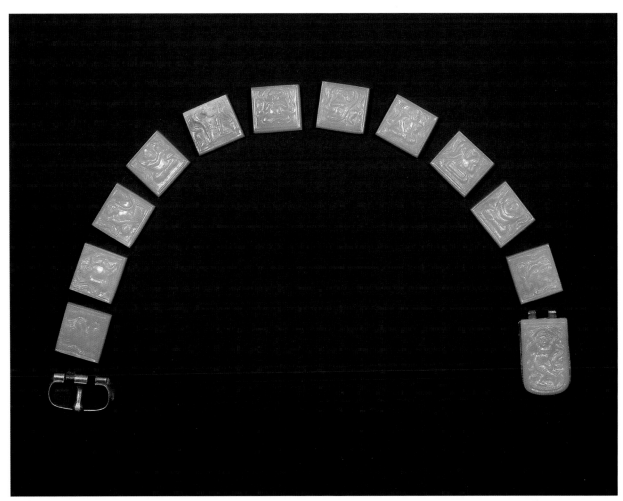

253

---

253   Belt with images of a musical troop

Tang
Length 45 cm
Width 3.4 cm

This belt, in greenish-white jade, consists of twelve pieces — eleven
square and one rectangular —and a copper belt hook. All are carved
with depictions of foreign musicians and dancers who have large eyes,
long hooked noses, various hairstyles and wearing short jackets with
narrow sleeves. The musicians sit on carpets playing various
instruments accompanying the dancers. Music and dance from
countries along the Silk Road west of China were very popular in the
Tang period. The jade pieces were originally mounted on a leather belt
and at the beginning of the Tang, the emperors, princes and all high
court officials wore jade belts like this. Hua Cixiang

254

254 Ring with dragon design
Tang
Diameter 9.6 cm

255

256

255 Deer
Song
Width 4.3 cm
Height 6.5 cm

256 Ornament with spring water images
Jin
Length 8.8 cm
Width 3.6 cm

257

257 Censer cover with lotus and egret design

Yuan

Height 5 cm, W: 4.6 cm

Excavated from Ren's tomb, Qingpu County, Shanghai, 1952.

This censer cover in green jade has egrets standing among openwork-carved lotus flowers, some looking for food and others on the verge of flight. This cover is used as a handle to lift the lid of the censer. In Chinese the words egret (*lu*) and lotus (*lian*) are homophones for the abbreviated form of the phrase '*yi lu lian ke*', which wishes scholars success in the imperial examinations. HUA CIXIANG

258 Plaque with dragon design

Ming

Length 3.4 cm

Width 2.6 cm

Excavated from Zhu Shoucheng's tomb, Baoshan County, Shanghai, 1966.

This rectangular plaque with the remains of a round handle on top is made from a white jade with a dragon and cloud design carved in shallow relief on both sides. It is an exquisitely carved ornament originally belonging one of the Ming literati. HUA CIXIANG

258

259

259 *Gu* with three dragon pattern

Qianlong reign period
Height 20.6 cm
Width 10.7 cm

This yellow jade *gu* has a lotus flower design at the top and bottom with coiled dragons carved in relief on the belly. The four character inscription, 'Made in the Qianlong reign period', is carved on the bottom in official script. The object's form emulates that of bronze ritual utensil of the Shang period. The Qianlong emperor advocated learning from the past and ordered jade craftsmen in the imperial court to make objects copying old forms. HUA CIXIANG

260 Mountain scene with human figures

Qing
Length 29.2 cm
Width 6.5 cm, Height 19 cm

260

8

MING AND QING FURNITURE

Although furniture is primarily for everyday use, its design, making and decoration often have aesthetic value. Classical Chinese furniture has clear artistic characteristics and a distinctive style, thus making it deserving of a place in the history of Chinese art and crafts.

Before the Han period people in China used to sit on the floor and furniture was low and lacked variety. Chairs started to be adopted during the Wei, Jin, Southern and Northern Dynasties periods, following interaction between China and countries along the Silk Road. Other varieties of furniture came with them. Both styles — sitting on the floor and sitting in chairs — continued through to the Tang period but by the Song chairs were dominant. Many types of higher level furniture were produced, with great variety of designs, and this laid the foundation for the furniture design in the Ming and Qing periods.

The mid and late Ming saw economic growth and expensive hardwoods, such as *huanghuali* (lit. Yellow flowering pear/plum) and *zitan* (lit. Purple rosewood), were used in furniture making. Chinese names for types of wood are often generic and therefore do not necessarily identify a single species. This was a period when many houses were built by the official classes and there was a demand for fine furniture, so that furniture making and design also flourished, with more varieties and better designs. The literati took a great interest in this and even wrote essays on furniture design and interior decoration.

Ming style furniture went out of fashion in the mid-Qing period and was replaced with a style that emphasized elaborate decoration and carving and the intermixing of different materials. Qing furniture is therefore characterized by its extravagance and luxury. LIU GANG

261

261 *Huanghuali* folding round-back chair

Ming
Seat: 70 × 46.5 cm
Height 112 cm
Donated by the Zhuang family.

This type of folding chair was the seat of honour in a Ming household, representing power and status. The round crest rail is made from five sections which are smoothly interconnected. The back splat is made from a frame and three carved panels. The top panel has an openwork carved design of a hornless dragon and the middle one has an openwork *qilin* design. All the joints are covered with cupronickel, which is both functional and decorative.
LIU GANG

262 *Huanghuali* clothes rack with phoenix design

Ming
Length 176 cm
Width 47.5 cm
Height 168.5 cm
Donated by the Zhuang family.

262

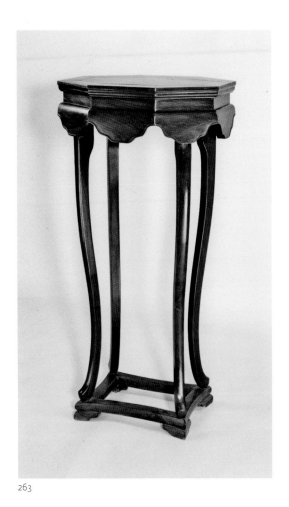

263

264

263 *Huanghuali* **four-legged octagonal incense table**
Ming
Surface of the stand 50.5 × 37.2 cm
Height 103 cm
Donated by the Zhuang family.

264 *Huanghuali* **'Southern Official's Hat Chair'**
Ming
Seat 58.5 × 47
Height 120 cm
Donated by the Zhuang family.

265

265 *Zitan* painting table
Ming
Length 190 cm
Width 74 cm
Height 78 cm
Donated by the Zhuang family.

This table belongs in the study and the *zitan* wood is dark and shiny from many years of use. The black lacquer floating panel is now cracked and spotted and has lost its sheen. The table has no waist. Its round legs are joined with stretchers and are without spandrels or braces making for a simple design typical of literati taste in this period.
LIU GANG

266 *Huanghuali* recessed-leg table with everted flanges
Ming
Length 140 cm
Width 28 cm
Height 87 cm
Donated by the Zhuang family.

266

267 *Huanghuali* bookcase
Ming
Length 98 cm
Width 46 cm, Height 177 cm
Donated by the Zhuang family.

268 *Huanghuali* high washbasin stand with carved decorations
Ming
Depth 60 cm
Height 176 cm
Donated by the Zhuang family.

267

268

269

269 Couch bed with *tieli* wood base and *zitan* wood three-panel screen railing
Ming
Width 221 cm
Depth 122 cm
Height 83 cm
Donated by the Zhuang family.

270 *Huanghuali* ceramic table screen
Qing
Width 67 cm
Depth 19 cm
Height 37 cm
Donated by Mrs Zhang De'an.

270

271

271 *Zitan* **imperial chair with cloud and dragon design**
Qing
Width 128 cm
Depth 89 cm
Total height 121 cm

272

272 *Zitan* **screen set on a wooden stand with engraved cloud and dragon design and jade inlay**
Qing
Width 375 cm
Depth 60 cm
Height 280 cm

This screen is typical of the mid-Qing period. It is extremely luxurious and sumptuous with decorations using various materials and techniques. The screen consists of five panels, engraved with dragons flying in clouds, birds, flowers, trees and rocks and with jade inlay. The screen stand is carved with a relief design of lotus-petals. The engraved and inlay work on this screen is superb, such exquisite workmanship symbolizing the emperor's power. LIU GANG

13

273

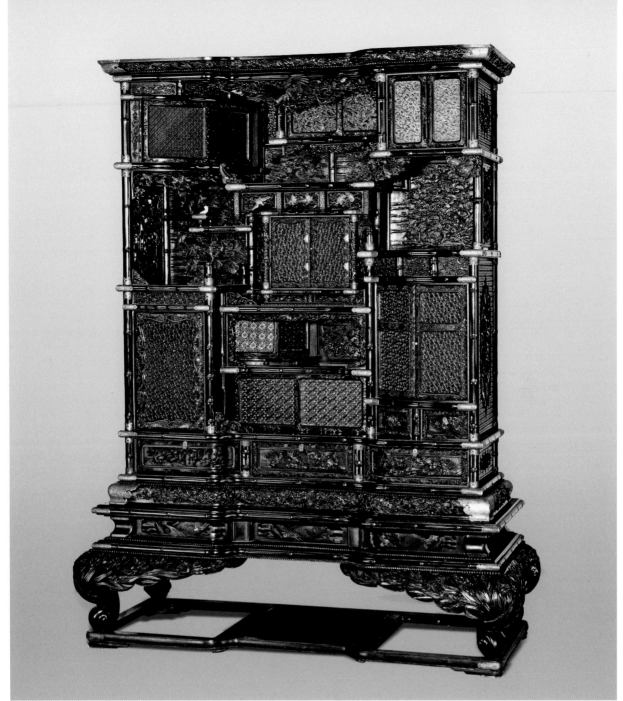

274

---

273 *Zitan* **armchair**

Qing

Seat 77 × 57.5 cm

Height 105.5 cm

---

274 *Zitan* **treasure shelf with bamboo and bird design**

Qing

Length 162 cm

Width 46 cm, Height 224 cm

9

China today is a country with many different peoples who have played an important role in the history and material culture of the region. There is great variety among these regional cultures, reflected in the artefacts, their colours and designs. This section includes pieces of art, religious artefacts, folk art and items for everyday use, including jewellery, clothes and textiles. Many of these preserve traditional techniques. Bao Yan Li

275

275 Court robe with gold embroidered cloud and dragon design
Manchu
Qing
Length 131.5 cm
Width 191 cm

276 Carved wooden hat stand
Bai, Dali, Yunnan Province
Qing
Height 30 cm

276

277

278

277 *Kapala* (skull) cup with
bronze lid and *Diamond Sutra*
dhāraṇi **inscription**
Tibetan
Qing
Length 16.2 cm
Width 13.3 cm
Height 25.6 cm

278 **Hair adornment of silver**
inlaid with coral beads
Mongol
Qing
Width 10 cm

279

279 Openwork bronze jar with a handle
Uighur, Xinjiang Uighur Autonomous
Region
First half of the 20th century
Diameter 18.4 cm, Height 40 cm

280 Hammered silver pot with legendary scenes

Dai, Menghai, Yunnan Province
First half of the 20th century
Diameter 10 cm
Height 9.4 cm

280

281

281 Shell-bead vest

Gaoshan, Taiwan
First half of the 20th century
Height 97 cm
Width 51 cm

The nobility of the Gaoshan ('High Mountain'), or original aboriginal inhabitants of Taiwan, used to wear clothes out of pierced shells as a symbol of wealth and status. A vest like this, which must be made of up to 100,000 tiny polished pierced shell-beads, is very labour intensive to make and is unique to this culture. BAO YAN LI

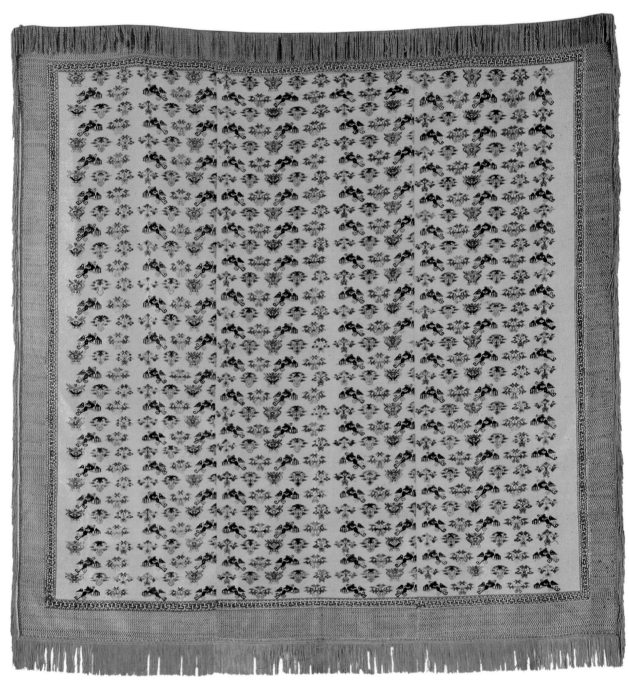

282

282 Table rug with bird, flower and tree patterns
Zhuang, Xinbin, Guangxi Province
Second half of the 20th century
296 × 148 cm

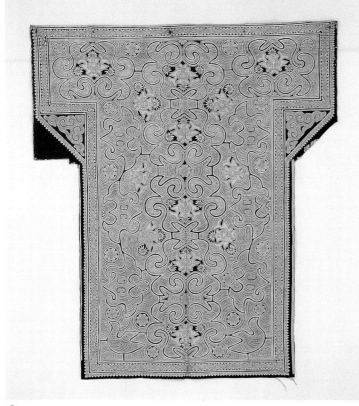

283

283

283 Batik baby sling with flower, butterfly and bird design

Miao, Huangping, Guizhou Province
Second half of the 20th century
77 × 68.5 cm

Batik is a technique over two thousand years old where wax is used to draw patterns on a piece of cloth before dyeing. After all the dyes have set the cloth is boiled to remove the wax and show the patterns. The batik produced in the Huangping region is very fine showing designs which combine natural elements with geometric patterns. BAO YAN LI

284 Shoulder bag embroidered with horse-tail hair entwined with white silk thread

Shui, Sandu, Guizhou Province
98 × 166 cm (with strap)

284

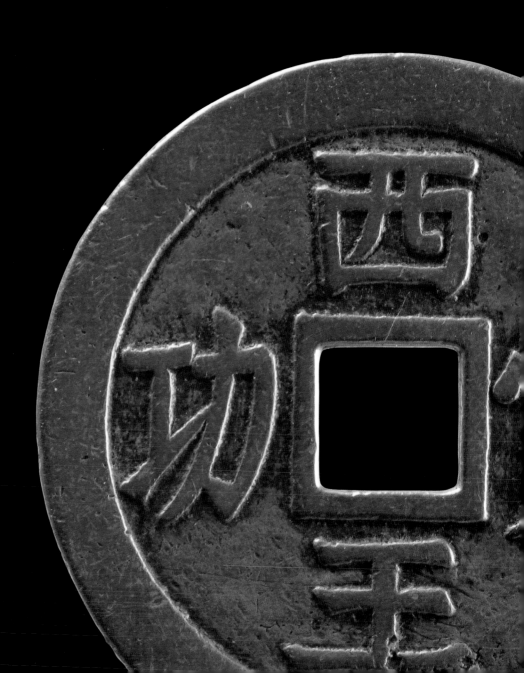

10

The Shanghai Museum coin collection, with over a million items, is said to represent half of the total numismatic collection of China. It is also renowned for its quality. The exhibits in the money gallery include old Chinese coins, modern machine-made paper money, old paper money, gold and silver ingots and other forms of currency, as well as the machinery for minting coins and printing banknotes. There are also special displays of gold, silver and copper coins from countries along the Silk Road, as well as coins that were issued for ceremonial use and not for general circulation.

Some of the coins are unique specimens: for example, the coin of the Yongle reign period of the Ming with the inscription '*san qian*' (three cash), and the gold coin with the inscription '*Xiwang shanggong*' (Reward of the Western King), issued by Zhang Xianzhong (1606–47), a Chinese rebel leader who ruled an area of southwest China in the 17th century. Many other well-known treasures include a Genghis Khan gold coin, a Jiangnan 20-cash coin issued in the *jiachen* year of the Guangxu reign (1904) and silver coins issued in Hubei and Sichuan during the Guangxu reign period of the Qing. ZHOU XIANG

285

285

285 Coin issued during Ming Yongle reign period (1403–25) with the inscription 'san qian' (three cash) on the reverse

Diameter 3.4 cm

286

286 Coin with inscription 'Xiwangang shanggong' issued under the rebel leader, Zhang Xianzhong (1606–57)

Diameter 5 cm

287

287 Twenty cash copper coin issued in Jiangnan in the *jiachen* year of the Guangxu reign period (1904)

Diameter 3.3 cm
Donated by Sun Ding.

288

288

288

289

289 1 *tael* silver coin minted in Guangdong Province with the inscription '*shou*'(longevity) c.1904–5

Diameter 4.2 cm

Donated by Wang Kangyuan.

290 Silver coins minted in Hubei Province during the Guangxu reign period (1875–1908)

Diameter 3.98 cm, 3.3 cm, 2.4 cm

Donated by Wang Kangyuan

290

290

290

288 Silver coins issued in Sichuan in the Guangxu reign period (1875–1908)

Diameters 3.98 cm, 3.3 cm, 2.4 cm

Largest coin donated by Li Weixian

Smallest coin donated by Wang Kangyuan

The three silver coins from the Sichuan mints are shown here are extremely rare. The denominations are given in both Chinese and English 7 *qian* 2 *fen* (7 mace 2 candareens), 3 *qian* 6 *fen* and 1 *qian* 4 *fen* 4 *li*. Although the size decreases with the smaller denominations, the design is the same for all three. Within the central circle on the obverse is the inscription '*Guangxu yuanbao*' (Guangxu currency) written in Chinese and Manchu. The inscription '*Sichuan sheng zao*' (made in Sichuan Province) is written around the upper edge, the denomination around the lower edge, and the two separated by six-pointed stars. At the centre of the reverse is an S-shaped dragon, with the inscription 'Szechuen Province' and the denomination, both given in English, written around the edge, separated again with six-pointed stars.

In a memorial submitted to the emperor on the 4th day of the 12th month of the 25th year of the Guangxu reign period (1899) the Sichuan Governor Kun Jun wrote: 'Your humble servant investigated the successive arrival in the 24th year (1898) of the machinery to mint silver and copper coins. The foreign technician also arrived. Managers were sent by the relevant departments and students were recruited. I have ordered them to install the equipment as soon as possible, as once the work started the foreign technician can return to his country... I have investigated the cost of the installation of the equipment, purchase of the bricks, wood, and other material, expenses of the foreign technician, managers, salaries of the managers and craftsmen, food etc, and the total expenditure from the 1st of the 4th month to the end of the 10th month of the 24th year of the Guangxu reign period is 2986 *liang* (taels) 4 *qian* 7 *fen* 4 *li* 9 *hao*.' The coins shown here must have been minted during this period on the machinery described. ZHOU XIANG

291

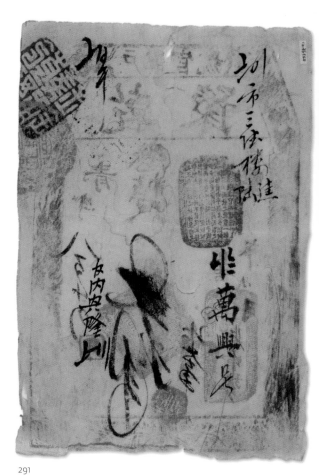

291

292

291 Bank cheque worth two thousand *wen* (cash) with official title '*qian yu*' from the Ministry of Finance, 1853

Length 17.85 cm, Width 12.5 cm

Donated by Wu Chouzhong.

292 1-*yuan* paper note issued in Guangxi Province dated the 30th year of the Guangxu reign period (1905)

Length 11.3 cm, Width 19.5 cm

Donated by Wu Chouzhong.

293 Silver coin issued under the Arsacid Parthian King, Phraataces (Phraates V) (r. 2 BC – AD 4)

Diameter 2.1 cm

Donated by Du Weishan and Tan Duanyan.

293   293

293

294   294

294 Gold coin of Genghis Khan

Diameter 2.4 cm, Weight 4.2 g

Donated by Du Weishan and Tan Duanyan.

Very few coins from Genghis Khan's Mongol Empire have survived, and it is extremely rare to see one like this, giving his full name, the place and date of minting. These coins followed the coinage of the Islamic tradition, with the inscriptions given in Arabic. The inscription on the obverse is taken from the Qu'ran. The inscription on the reverse reads: 'This coin was minted at Ghazni in AH 618 (AD 1221)', with the issuer's name written inside the circle: 'The Khan of all Khans, the greatest, the most just, Genghis Khan'. This coin was minted to celebrate the victory of Genghis Khan's army over the King of Khwarezm in 1221. WANG YUE

11

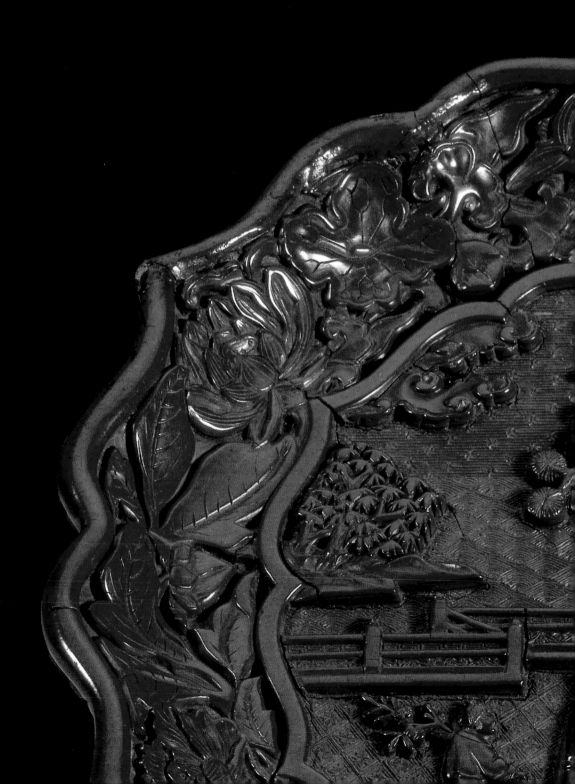

China was one of the earliest civilisations to produce lacquer ware. A seven thousand year old red lacquer bowl has been excavated from the early Neolithic Hemudu site at Yuyao, Zhejiang Province. During the Shang and the Zhou periods, there was a great leap in lacquer production and it reached a peak in the Warring States to Han periods. Numerous lacquers were produced in a very highly structured industry where there were skilled workers for the different stages of production. New forms were developed but they were still largely utilitarian. This gradually changed after the Han and lacquers became seen as aesthetic as well as functional objects. Many new forms were developed along with techniques such as carving and the use of silver and gold, and mother-of-pearl inlay.

The art continued during the Yuan, Ming and Qing periods when individual craftsmen produced their own works and the wares started to gain the attention of the imperial court. Imperial and local lacquer workshops existed side by side, developed together and created many masterpieces. BAO YAN LI

295

295 Carved red circular box with image of picking chrysanthemums

Yuan

Diameter 12 cm

Height 3.9 cm

Excavated at the Ren Tomb, Qingpu County, Shanghai, 1952.

Carved black lacquer wares are typical of the Yuan period but this is the only excavated piece of carved red lacquer. The design refers to a poem by Tao Yuanming (365–427) with the lines 'picking chrysanthemums by the eastern fence, gazing at the Southern mountains.' BAO YAN LI

296

296 Carved red dish with flycatchers (*shoudai*) and peonies
Ming
Diameter 31.3 cm
Height 3.8 cm

297 Carved red water chestnut shaped dish with design of returning home
Yongle reign period, Ming (1403–1424)
Diameter 18.8 cm
Height 3 cm

297

**298 Carved red circular box
with cloud and dragon design**
Xuande reign period, Ming
Diameter 15.2 cm
Height 6.6 cm

**299 Gold painted rectangular
dish with figurative painting**
Late Ming period (16th – 17th century)
Length 44.7 cm
Width 30.6 cm, Height 4.7 cm
Donated by Gu Lijiang.

298

299

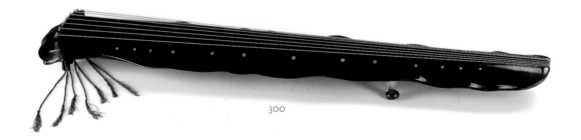

300

301 Octagon box with tray

Qing Yongzheng, 2nd Year 1724
Tray width 27.2 cm, Box width: 24.4 cm, Total height 31 cm

This octagonal box sits on its own tray and contains six fruit containers. Its sides are woven from thin bamboo strips. The lid is painted in gold with an image of a well-known motif, the Daoist Ma Gu along with the Eight Immortals congratulating the God of Longevity on his birthday. Hornless dragons are painted on the feet and the tray has the motif of bats. A gilt inscription on the inside of the lid and on the inside bottom of the box reads 'Made for Yang Chunfang'. On both the bottom of the box and the tray is the inscription 'Made for the use of Yang Chunfang in the summer of the *jiachen* year of the Yongzheng reign period of the great Qing Dynasty (1724).' BAO YAN LI

301

300 Musical instrument with inscription 'lu tian feng yu' (blue sky with wind and rain)

Ming
Length 120 cm, Width 20 cm
Depth 10.9 cm
Donated by Wu Jinxiang.

302

302 Black pavilion-shaped sutra shelf with inlaid mother-of-pearl

Mid-Qing period (18th century)
Length 35 cm
Width 21 cm
Height 31 cm

303 Black sunflower shaped dish with images of figures in a landscape in inlaid mother-of-pearl

Mid-Qing period (18th century)
Diameter 11.6 cm
Thickness 1.4 cm

303

304

304 Multi-coloured bodiless lacquer sculpture by Shen Zhenggao of the legendary turtle bearing peaches

2nd year of the Xuantong reign period (1910)

Height 66.7 cm

Donated by Shen Zhenggao.

12

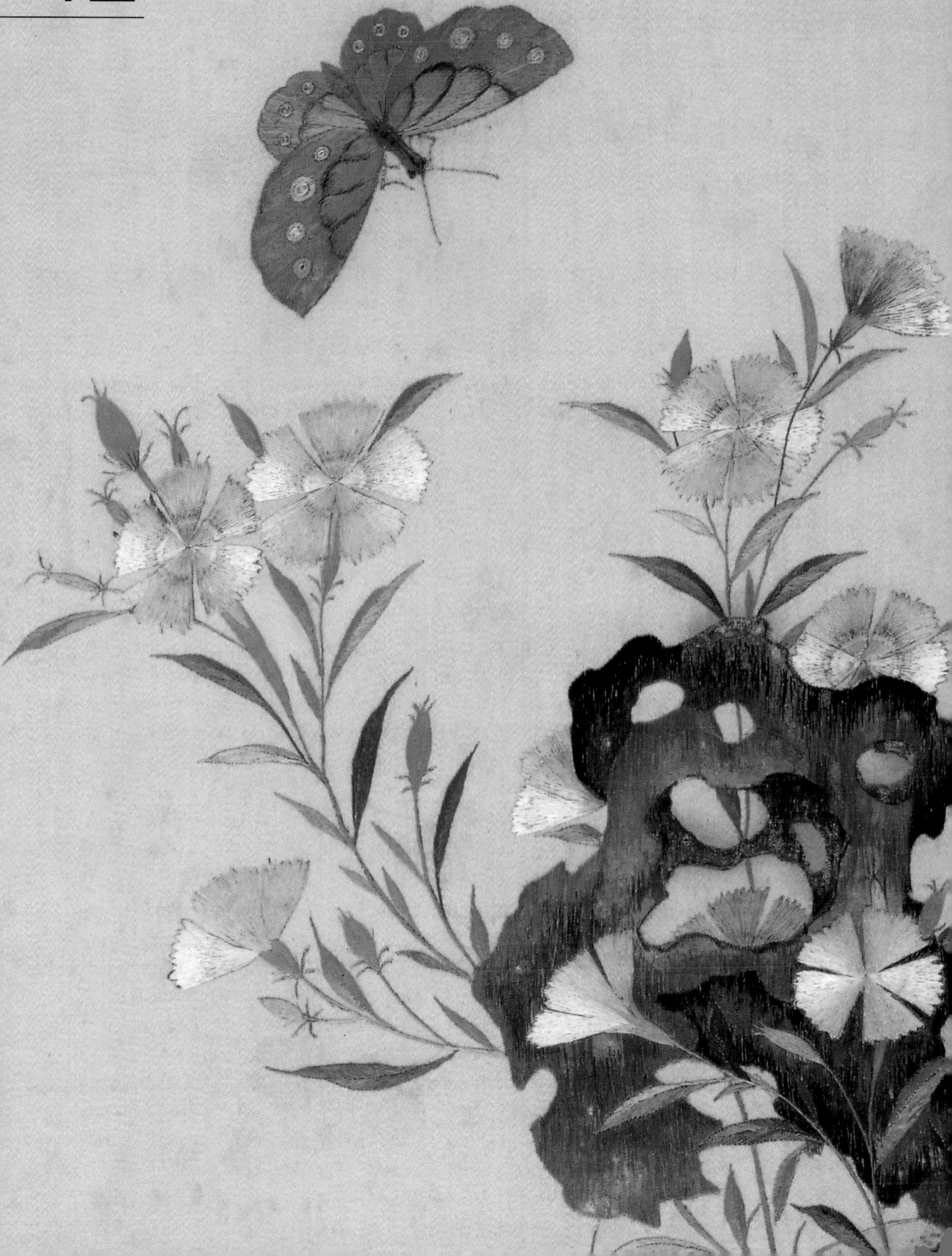

TAPESTRY AND EMBROIDERY

Tapestry is a weft faced weave with one warp and one weft which was in use in China by the Tang period, with early examples found in the Silk Road tombs near Turfan, Xinjiang. The pattern is woven using the weft threads on a beige warp but, unlike earlier textiles, the weft threads are not threaded through from selvedge to selvedge but only as far as the design, then turn back on themselves. Short slits are therefore left at the edge of the design and both sides of the tapestry are the same.

As a result of the development and popularity of painting in the Song period, weavers started to produce silk tapestry pictures closely copying the style of contemporary paintings. A group of outstanding tapestry artists appeared, among them Zhu Kerou. Silk tapestry remained popular through to the Ming and the Qing periods, when new techniques developed, such as combining silk tapestry with embroidery and painting.

Embroidery is an ancient Chinese craft. Records place its invention during the period of the mythical rulers Shun and Yao four to five thousand years ago. The earliest piece found to date was excavated from the Shang period Fuhao tomb at the Yinxu site, Henan Province. Before the Tang period, embroidery was mainly on everyday items. But, like tapestry, influenced by the development of painting in the Song period embroidery pictures started to be produced. A range of stitches were developed which could emulate paintings in their variations and shading of colours, and many embroideries are quite stunning.

Embroidery developed further in the Ming period with the Gu school — named after Gu Mingshi, head of an embroidery family from Shanghai. Han Mengxi, wife of his second grandson, refined the technique by combining painting with her embroidery skills.

There were four famous regional schools of embroidery in the Qing: Su embroidery from Suzhou: Xiang embroidery from Changsha, Hunan; Shu embroidery of Chengdu, Sichuan; and Yue embroidery from Guangzhou. Shen Shou was from the Su School and she used both Chinese and western painting techniques as a blueprint for her visually stunning embroidery pictures. ZHANG QINGYUN

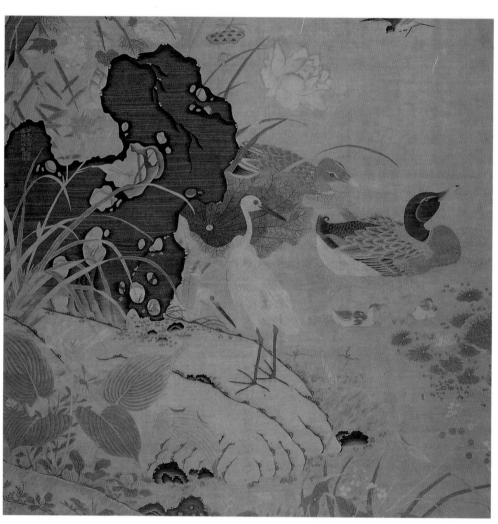

305

305 Silk tapestry
Zhu Kerou (12th century)
Northern Song
Height 107.5 cm
Width 108.8 cm

Zhu Kerou, style name Gang, was from Yunjian in Jiangdong (present-day Songjiang in Shanghai) and was active in the twelfth century. She was considered the leading tapestry weaver of her age. This piece is typical of her work, with a colourful design of a duck and her ducklings swimming among the lotus flowers. The scene also shows other aquatic plants and birds. It bears a silk inscription of 'Lotus pond and ducklings by Zhu Gang of Jiangdong' and a seal with the inscription 'Kerou'. ZHANG QINGYUN

306

306   Silk tapestry depicting immortals congratulating the God of Longevity on his birthday
Ming
Height 164 cm
Width 118 cm

307   Silk tapestry of birds and flowers
Qianlong reign period, Qing
Height 77.2 cm
Width 95 cm

307

308

308   Silk tapestry of pheasants and camellias
Qing
Height 120.5 cm
Width 60.6 cm

309   Silk tapestry of female immortals on the river
Qing
Height 82.7 cm
Width 43.8 cm
Donated by Pang Bingli.

310   Silk embroidery of Buddha from the Anxi Palace
The 7th year of the Chenghua reign period, Ming (1471)
Height 93.2 cm
Width 31 cm

309

310

311

312

311 *Gu* silk embroidery of East Mountain

Late Ming period (16th – 17th century)
Length 79.5 cm
Width 27.1 cm

312 *Gu* silk embroidery of a lake with rocks, flowers and butterflies

Han Ximeng (active early 17th century)
Late Ming Period
Height 30.3 cm
Width 23.9 cm

313

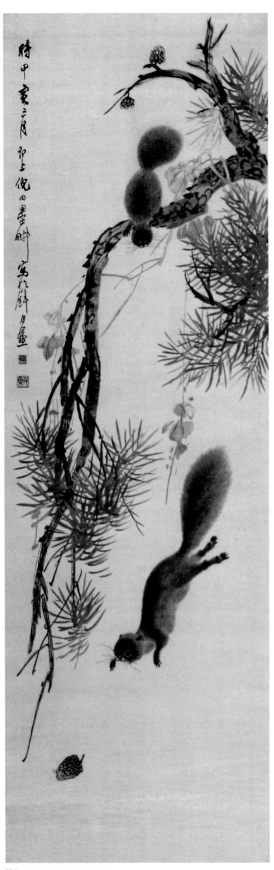

314

313 Silk embroidery of flowers and bird

Shen Shou (active late 19th – early 20th century)
Qing
Height 42 cm
Width 15 cm

Shen Shou was from Suzhou and a famous embroiderer of the late Qing period. Her 'Portrait of Jesus' won first prize in the Panama World Expo held at San Francisco in 1915. Although the stitching is not complicated on the work shown here it is still a skilful piece. The stitches are almost invisible and the edges so neat that it closely resembles a painting. It bears the seal 'Madame Shen' on the lower right hand corner.
ZHANG QING YUN

314 Silk embroidery copy of Ni Mogeng's (1855–1919) painting of squirrels

Qing
Height 127.5 cm
Width 41 cm

13

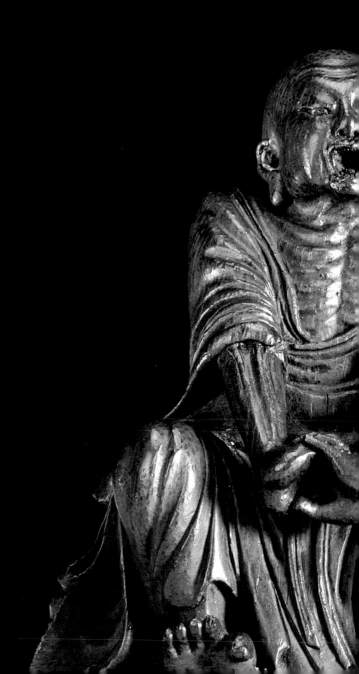

BAMBOO, WOOD, IVORY AND RHINOCEROS HORN CARVINGS

Making sculpture out of natural materials such as bamboo, wood, ivory and rhinoceros horn has long been a part of Chinese culture but these arts flourished in the late imperial period, building on older traditions from the Song and Yuan periods. This was a time when the literati had wealth and leisure, and they focussed much of this on aesthetic activities. Not only were they collectors, but many also became skilled carvers themselves. The imperial court also commissioned many such objects, setting the highest standards in materials and craftsmanship. Bamboo, wood, ivory and rhinoceros horn carvings thus reached a golden era, many schools formed and master craftsmen emerged. Craftsmen were often skilled in working in all four media, although carvings from each had their own characteristics. SHI YUAN

315

315 Bamboo incense holder carved

Zhu Ying 1520–87
Ming
Height 16.5 cm
Diameter 3.7 cm
Excavated from the tomb of Zhu Shoucheng and his wife,
Baoshan, Shanghai, 1966

This incense holder was carved by the artist Zhu Ying and
shows a scene from a famous collection of mystery and
ghost stories dating back to the Six Dynasties period,
Youminglu (A Record of the Seen and Unseen). This depicts a
story about two Eastern Han figures, Liu Chen and Ruan
Zhao, who visited Mount Tiantai and encountered beautiful
women, who are immortals. This fable — scholars meeting
beautiful female immortals — has become a paradigm love
story. Here the artist concentrated on showing the
comfortable and leisurely life of the immortals.

This object is carved in many layers using several
techniques, among them openwork (allowing escape of the
fragrant smoke), intaglio and high-relief. It also uses a
technique known as *liuqing* (reserve-green), a type of
shallow relief engraving that exploits the contrasting colors
and textures of the smooth greenish bamboo skin and the
darker, more fibrous inner layer of the stalk. The design is cut
from the lighter skin and stands in relief against the ground.
It is a rare treasure of the Chinese bamboo carving.
SHI YUAN

316 Bamboo brush pot engraved with figures reading in a garden

Shen Dasheng (active 17th century)
Ming
Mouth 13.1 × 15.5 cm
Height 14.9 cm

316

317

317 Bamboo brush pot engraved

Wu Zhifan (active 1662 – 1722)
Height 15.4 cm
Qing
Diameter of mouth 12.3 cm
Diameter of base: 12.6 cm

The image on this brush pot shows the Qiao sisters, characters in the famous 14th century historical novel, *Sanguo yanyi* (The Romance of the Three Kingdoms). The figures and all other details are carved in great detail using a technique where the background has been carved away to make the image more prominent. Wu Zhifan specialised in this technique. SHI YUAN

318

**318 Statue of *arhat* carved
from bamboo root**
Feng Xilu (active early 18th century)
Qing
Width 12.2 cm
Height 15 cm

319

320

321

319 Brush pot with engraving of chrysanthemum and rocks using the 'reserve-green' (*liuqing*) technique

Pan Xifeng 1736–95
The 4th year of the Yongzheng reign period,
Qing (1726)
Height 10.2 cm
Diameter 6.3 cm

320 Brush pot with engraving of buildings and landscape using the 'reserve-green' (*liuqing*) technique

Zhang Xihuang (active early 17th century)
Qing
Height 10.3 cm
Diameter of mouth 5.9 cm
Diameter of base: 5.8 cm
Donated by Chen Qicheng.

321 Bamboo brush pot engraved with bamboo and rocks

Zhou Hao (1675–1763)
8th year of the Qianlong reign period,
Qing (1743)
Height 14.8 cm
Diameter of mouth 8.9 cm
Diameter of base: 9.1 cm

322

323

322 The poet Tao Yuanming admiring chrysanthemum carved from bamboo root
Deng Fujia (active early 18th century)
Qing
Width 6.9 cm
Height 14.3 cm

323 Bamboo wrist-rest engraved with two immortals crossing a river
Deng Wei (active mid 18th century –
beginning. 19th century)
Qing
Length 22.7 cm
Width 7.6 cm

324 The drunken poet Li Bo carved from bamboo root
Cai Shimin (active late 18th century)
Qing
Height 9.1 cm

325 Bamboo root pot engraved with auspicious designs of bats and peaches
Qing
Length 29 cm
Width 15.5 cm
Height 11.5 cm

324

325

326

326 Miniature mountain with immortals carved from bamboo root

Qing

Height 30 cm

Width 19.5 cm

Donated by Pan Huiyin.

327 Bamboo carved wine vessel with a handle
Qing
Height 27.5 cm
Base 14 × 11.1 cm
Body 17 × 14.4 cm

328 Statue of Dongfang Shuo carved from *huangyang* wood
Qing
Height 15.3 cm
Width 5.4 cm

328

327

329

329 Statue of Ji Gong carved from *huangyang* wood
Zhu Zichang (active late 19th – early 20th century)
Qing
Height 17.3 cm

330 Carved rhinoceros horn raft cup
Bao Tiancheng (active 17th century)
Qing
Length 25.5 cm
Width 9.9 cm
Height 9.7 cm

This raft-shaped cup depicts the famous Han imperial envoy, Zhang Qian, who was sent to the western regions: his visit led to the development of Chinese trade along the Silk Road. Bao Tiancheng was an eminent rhinoceros horn carver of the Ming period. His work covered a variety of subjects including figures and flowers and plants. BAO YAN LI

331

331 Ivory carving of a cabbage with insects
Late Qing period (Early 20th century)
Length 25 cm

330

332

332 Rhinoceros horn cup with six dragons
You Kan (active 1660–1720)
Qing
Mouth 11.4 × 16.2 cm
Height 9.2 cm

333 Rhinoceros horn cup with openwork flower and dragon design
Late Ming (16th – 17th century)
Mouth 15.4 × 10.6 cm
Height 23.7 cm

333 >

334

**334 Rhinoceros horn square
ding (food container) with
animal masks**
Mid-Qing (18th century)
Length 10.8 cm
Width 8.1 cm
Height 18.4 cm